Stories Dad Told Me

~

Manny Azenberg's Adventures in Life and the Theatre

Jessica Azenberg

ISBN: 978-0-578-29826-9

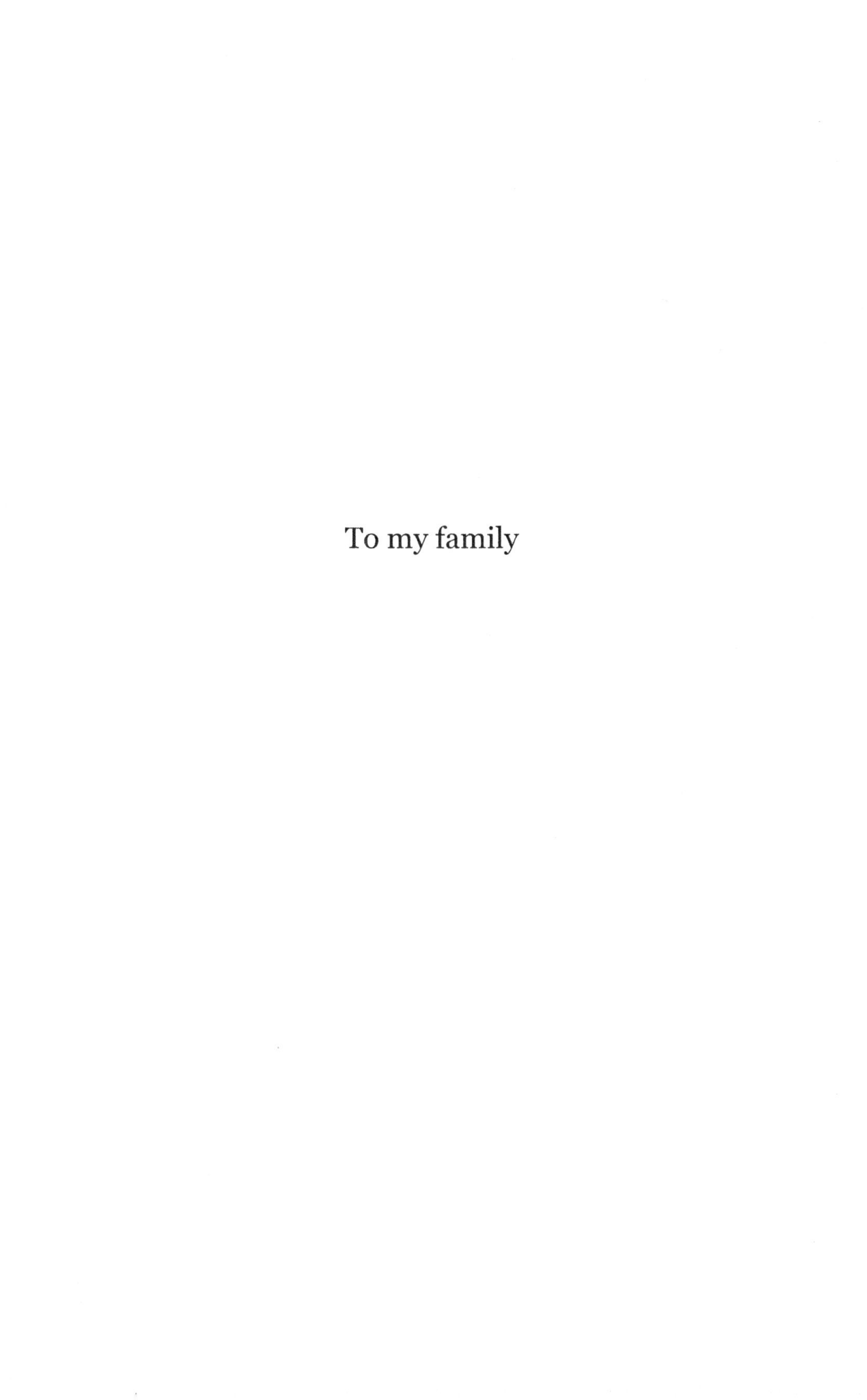

To my family

CONTENTS

INTRODUCTION

My dad always says the opening number of a Broadway show should tell the audience what the next two hours of the evening is going to be about. So here goes...

My dad tells good stories. I also think he's very funny. He usually tells his stories around the dinner table or in the living room. Sometimes he tells them in front of friends and sometimes he shares them with his family. I have heard some stories multiple times and others I've heard only once. A few years ago, I decided these stories needed to be written down. I wanted to be able to share them with my present and future family. I knew his stories were wonderful and they needed to live on, but I had no idea when some of the events he described had happened. So, I asked if I could sit down with him and record him talking.

My dad is a natural storyteller. It's how he communicates. All these stories, put together, tell the story of his life. We ended up talking for hours and hours, over a period of five years, after which I transcribed everything he had said, line by line. During that process, I felt I was hearing the stories again. Writing this book was like going back in time and reliving my father's past, being there with him when he was in the Army or at his summer camp.

I have never felt closer to my father than I did while writing this book. I now feel more in touch with my Jewish heritage and where I come from. I understand the importance of family and continuing traditions in ways I could not have imagined before. I also learned how much we have in common. I learned that I've inherited my managerial ability from my father as well as my mother.

Not only did I get to relive his wonderful stories, but I also discovered the importance of the values he absorbed throughout his life. My dad often talks about "behaving well." He has earned his reputation and success in the theatre business because he is kind, smart, and loyal. He doesn't cheat, and he behaves well.

This book is not about who my father knows, or how many shows he has produced. It's not about exposing anyone he has worked with. It's not about the "glamorous life" of a Broadway producer. And it's not about people's preconceived idea of the life of a Broadway producer's daughter. I never grew up "backstage," surrounded by Broadway stars. I'm grateful that I grew up in a household with good values, which my father and I share, and I hope this book will convey the same values to all who read it.

I love you, Dad.

1 THE BRONX

I was born in the Bronx in 1934, at 1235 Grand Concourse on 167th Street. I don't remember anything about that... And then we moved to 760 Grand Concourse when my sister, Cookie, was born. We shared a room. I looked at that building fifty years later, and it's a small six-story building. I think my father, Charlie, once said he lived on Rivington Street on the Lower East Side and in Harlem and then moved up to the Bronx.

I went to PS 35 on Morris Avenue at 163rd Street, which went to the sixth grade, and was across the street from St. Angela's Catholic School. We were very wary of all the Catholic kids because they would beat up on all the Jewish kids. We learned to bless ourselves as we walked in front of St. Angela's, so nobody bothered us because they thought we were Catholic. Almost everybody in our apartment building was Jewish, except for Louie Corahias who was Greek, and Ina Rasmussen who was Scandinavian. There were a few Irish families as well. There was Genie and Johnny Loughlin who were Irish. They were two of ten Loughlin kids who lived in the same building and were the toughest kids in the neighborhood. We hung out and stayed in our own neighborhood which was six apartment buildings.

You have to understand that we didn't leave the Bronx. We stayed in the Bronx. We did everything in the Bronx. We went to school and to the movies in the Bronx. There were Kosher delicatessens every six blocks or so, and for 25 cents you got rolled beef on a plate with French fries. Don't ask what rolled beef was, but for 35 cents you got roast beef. You could eat lunch for 40 cents and an entire pizza cost 75 cents. In our neighborhood, you were always part of a club, and later some of those clubs became gangs. We had jackets and everybody wore their club jacket. I wish I had that jacket. I would give it to you.

I was a good student, but occasionally I'd cut school with my friends and see a movie instead of going to class. The movies on a Saturday afternoon in the Bronx cost 17 cents and Jujubes cost 5 cents. You watched two movies and a cartoon. People smoked in the movies in those days—it must have killed a lot of them. You smoked Chesterfields or Camels or Lucky Strikes if you were macho.

When you were sixteen or seventeen, you wanted to bring a girl and neck in the back of the movie theatre. A heavy date meant going downtown on the subway to Manhattan to see a movie at the Roxy or the Paramount. You could see a stage show with Frank Sinatra or Tommy Dorsey or Danny Kaye, followed by a movie—that cost a dollar and a quarter. Then you took the girl for spaghetti and meatballs at a 47th Street restaurant for 85 cents a plate. That was a 5-dollar date—that was a heavy date. Wow, you better marry that girl!

You grew up on the streets in those days in the Bronx. You came home from school, threw your books in your room, put your sneakers on, ran downstairs two at a time, and played games on the streets. When it snowed, we threw snowballs, and we did what we called "sleigh riding," which was really sledding down the hills. We also played stickball, with a pink rubber ball and a broomstick. We played games called slug, king, hit the curb, skelly, immies. It was very creative. We even built a basketball court with peach baskets. We had another game in the park that we called "capture the white flag." You had to create your own games.

As we got a little older, we played basketball and softball in Macombs Dam Park near Yankee Stadium, where there were ball fields. You had to be a Yankee fan, or you'd be assassinated—I lived four blocks from the stadium. Basketball was played on concrete. I was realistic enough to know that I wasn't going to be a baseball or basketball player, but I loved playing basketball more than anything. I miss it now. I was a good school yard ball player.

We didn't play football—I was too small anyway—but we played softball in camp and basketball forever. My parents knew nothing about baseball, softball, or basketball. It was mysterious to them. Why would anybody waste their time? Red Holzman, who was a pro basketball player and the coach of the New York Knicks, was a friend—not then but later. He would describe playing basketball with Yiddish-speaking immigrant parents. He would throw his sneakers out of the window so his parents wouldn't see them. Then he would run downstairs, pick them up, and go play basketball.

I had a classic Bronx upbringing. There was always food, and you ate what was on your plate. I don't remember steak, but I do remember meatloaf. I didn't think we were poor, but all our clothes came from discount stores. There's a moment in *Brighton Beach Memoirs*, when Matthew Broderick's character, Eugene, says to the father, "I need some sneakers. I've taped them."

That's what we did. Why? Because we bought sneakers and then our feet grew, so we cut out the toes and put tape on to cover the holes. We listened to Classical music and there were concerts—with Toscanini conducting—on the radio. My mother played Chopin on the piano, and we had to tiptoe around the house. I hated Chopin until I was about thirty.

We were aware of the need for an education. For a Jewish identity, you went to Hebrew school and to the synagogue on the high holidays. I had my Bar Mitzvah in an Orthodox synagogue. Literature wasn't imposed on us, but it was sitting right there on the bookshelf—Dickens, Mark Twain, Thackeray... And during my father's eulogy, his half-brother David said that when they all came from Europe, Charlie gave them reading lists. They had to read all of Dickens and all of Thackeray. We grew up in a world in which a certain kind of culture was extended to us, with books and Classical music.

We also had to get decent grades in school, or our father wanted to know why. I did not get good grades in math, ever. It was always difficult. If I got a 75, I was grateful, and I didn't really care about science. I got better grades in English and History. There was a serious discussion about why I didn't want to be a doctor, which was a huge disappointment to my parents. It's always a big joke ("be a doctor, be a doctor") but for my parents that meant success and stability. I might have been a lawyer, but we had to put down what our future interest was when we were sixteen years old. When I applied to college at seventeen, I might have put down pre-law just because it was something definitive, but I turned out to be an English major.

In terms of an American experience, it was probably healthy. There was food, everybody had jobs, and if you wanted extra money then you delivered clothes from the tailor or food from the grocer. You made 75 cents an hour doing something. From age fifteen on, almost everybody had a job after school, certainly in the summer, and you became a little bit more independent because if you wanted to go on a date and you were sixteen, you'd better have a few dollars.

We were too young to deal with the Depression, but we grew up during World War II. During the war, meat was rationed. Maybe that's when I learned to like liver, which nobody else seems to like. Serving your country was automatic and that's why people said, "I'm going into the service."

The older guys went into the Army, and everyone was truly patriotic. During the Vietnam War, things were different, and people left the country and consciously chose to move to Canada. Nobody did that in World War II or during the Korean War. World War II galvanized everyone. Those who were in the service would be away for years. Many were killed and all became neighborhood heroes. The tribal bigotry between Jews, Irish, and Italian gangs or clubs began to diminish. There were too many young men in uniform focused on a real enemy, and the violent but petty differences among our Bronx tribes became much less important.

Nevertheless, we wanted to get out of the Bronx. It was chic to live in Manhattan or date a girl from Manhattan. I don't think the parents of the Manhattan girls wanted the Bronx boys to go out with their daughters, but I guess it would have been alright if they were going to be doctors. Almost everybody had two parents. Whether they liked each other or not, it didn't matter. There was a real foundation here and purpose. You didn't waste any money because your parents didn't have any.

My childhood had the pluses of growing up in a lower middle-class Bronx place that had a built-in value system. Some of it may have been Victorian, but there was a value system.

There's a line in *Brighton Beach Memoirs* or one of the plays, where one of the brothers goes, "Oh shit!"

And the mother says, "WHAT did you say?!"

It was so truthful. You didn't swear at home. What you said on the street, you didn't say in your house. So there was a built-in value system about money, and a built-in value system about your behavior, and we didn't know how much it was worth at the time.

Included in the value system was what it meant to be Jewish in America, and in New York, because there was antisemitism here as well. Colleges had "Jew quotas," Park Avenue and Fifth Avenue had apartment houses that would not rent to Jews, and even as kids we were aware of the bigotry because it showed up on the streets of the Bronx. Also, you learned what it meant to be the first person in your family to have a college education. Well, certainly an American college education—the Rabbis had some other education.

As first-generation Americans, we moved from the Grand Concourse to 711 Walton Avenue, which was a step up. We paid 29 dollars more for rent and Cookie got her own room. If you add all of that up, we were participating in the American Dream. The pitfalls we found out about later, but we had to earn a living.

[Speaking to me] It's *your* tradition too. My father didn't cheat, and he didn't hustle. We don't do that. Did I ever tell you that I played basketball in college as a freshman with a Black guy named George Fox? The Jewish fraternity, Tau Delta Phi, wanted to pledge me, and I slept there for a couple of nights. I was thinking that I was ultimately not a fraternity guy, but I mentioned it to my father. I also mentioned that they didn't take "Negroes" and they didn't take George, with whom my father knew I played basketball.

My father didn't know any Black people, but he said, "No. Well, then you don't join."

It wasn't an argument. It wasn't a big speech. He just said, "No. You don't do that."

That was built in.

So you got something, and you could reject it. But there were virtues and assets that were present and those, at least in my life, turned out to be good things. For the most part with the people in the theatre, and I think you have discovered it also, I had a decent reputation for behaving well. I didn't cheat anybody. We don't do that.

There's now a street named "Manny Azenberg Way" in the Bronx, about four blocks from where I grew up. Your brother, Josh, pulled the curtain to reveal the sign. It's kind of a highlight because I thought if my father saw the name "Azenberg" somewhere on the Grand Concourse in the Bronx, he would approve and be proud.

That's it. I can't think of anything else.

2 KINDERWELT

Every summer that I can remember, we went to camp. It was a Zionist camp for adults and children. It was called Unser Camp and Kinderwelt. *Unser* in Yiddish means "our" and *Kinderwelt* means "children's world." It was a left-wing regular camp for children and a getaway for adults. It's not that the food was great, or the facilities were great, but it was paradise. You looked forward to the summer as if it were heaven. I went there as a camper and then as a counselor.

I don't know why, but many people who went there felt the same way. I can only conjecture what that camp experience meant to them. I don't think it was limited to Kinderwelt because other children also had that special summer camp experience. There were people you didn't see all year but only saw in the summer. When you were old enough, you dated. Bronx guys dated Brooklyn girls, and the reverse, which was like dating somebody from Chicago. Many people got married from that group. I think some of it had to do with the fact that you were with your own kind. You know that line from *West Side Story*? "Stick to your own kind." You didn't have school, you didn't have antisemitism, and you didn't have the complications of the streets of New York. I think I went there every summer from the age of four until I was twenty. When I was twenty, I went to boot camp for the Army and then came up for the last four weeks of the summer, and that was it.

People had great names—like Pee Wee Benditovich, Blackie Pfeffer, Whitey Arkush, Jughead Birnbaum, Cannonball Kalinsky, Moishe Mel Glick, Lemon Warshawsky, Sholom Secunda, and Lazar Weiner. It was not at all religious, but it was culturally Jewish, and it was a great escape. It was also *definitively* Zionist. The camp existed before World War II, and almost everybody's parents were born in Europe, and everybody was a first-generation American. Kinderwelt defined a kind of "being Jewish without being religious" and it was the great innocent period of my life. It was spectacular. You played basketball, you played baseball, and you swam. It lasted two months and then everybody left.

My sister and I stayed longer because our father was the camp manager. Sometimes we went back to school late because he had to stay up there. It was September and the crickets... It was the woods... It was the country... It was something you didn't experience in the Bronx, and it was a separate life experience from anything in New York. It was only fifty miles out of the city, but in those days fifty miles out of New York was like "on the moon." In the late forties and early fifties, very few people had a car, so once you were there, you had nowhere else to go. The camp has been closed for forty years now, but I think if you talk to those who went, they'll have a similar response. I don't know what the contemporary experience is now. Kids go to camp and I'm sure it's wonderful, but this had something else.

It was probably the most unencumbered experience of my life. One not filled with political problems, social problems, marital problems, or children's problems. It was cultural. There was a Yiddish culture, a Zionist culture, and the arts. Some of the people who worked there went on to become well-known artists—Sidney Lumet, who became a film producer, and his father Baruch Lumet, was an actor there. A guy who wrote a Broadway show and died—Steven Vinaver. The great sculptor, Chaim Gross, was the arts and crafts guy. So that was somewhat of a seminal experience. It's where my Zionist education came from. I don't know what contemporary people look back on as their seminal experience. We certainly remember the schools we went to because we went to them, but we remember Kinderwelt because it was wonderful and probably an escape.

There were some terrific athletes there. My recollection is that I played basketball for six hours a day on a court that had pebbles on it. The facilities were not good. There were no nets, but there were chains. The expression in those days was if you scored a basket, it was "swish." Not up there. It was "clang." You put on shows in English and in Yiddish too. You made lifetime friends because the people you knew at Kinderwelt, you couldn't posture with ten or twenty years later—no matter who you pretended to be, you were still a schlepper from bunk twelve. To quote Tom Stoppard, "You had to be there."

It was probably psychologically a very important part of my life. Every Saturday there was a dramatic show. At the end of breakfast, Sholom Secunda played the piano and led us all in songs, most of them in Hebrew and some in Yiddish. There was a band there. And at night, the older kids and counselors went down to what we called the "Casino," which was like a club, and there was folk dancing as well as social dancing. You participated in dances that you wouldn't dare do in the city but up there it was okay. You obviously did the hora, but you did Russian Shers and troikas too. You had a girlfriend every summer. I was about fourteen or fifteen and it was Sandra Fleming. When I was sixteen or seventeen, there were two girls named Fran Frost and Florence Bromberg. You could say it was very Victorian dating, or at least I thought so. Maybe other stuff went on that I didn't know about, but it was a lot of innocence, and when you escaped from the city, you escaped from everything.

Being the manager of the camp, and managing all those Jews, was not so easy for my father, but he was a respected gentleman, and he ran it well. It was one of those Jewish organizations where everybody was self-important, and he had to put up with all of that. He actually had to run the place. I think the town made my father an honorary sheriff of Sullivan County because he was an honorable man and tried to use all the local people and services to maintain the camp. He had no prejudice, and he paid the bills. Maybe my managerial ability comes from that, but he ran it for about twenty years, and it was very classy.

I think he ran a place before, called Camp Boiberik near Hyde

Park, and then they brought him down to run Kinderwelt. That was his main job, as far as I know. He probably came to Kinderwelt in about 1938, stayed until 1954 or '55, and retired. Remember, my father was born in 1894, so by 1954 he was sixty. My parents bought a house, a little cottage in a summer colony next to the camp called Raanana. We would go up, my first wife and me. I even took your mother up there in the early spring to pick wild strawberries. The camp no longer exists, and it is now a tract of homes. The camp was bulldozed.

You know our house in Connecticut when we walk to the tennis court, that little path? I think of it as the path that I walked on the way to the dining room in Kinderwelt. It's just nothing but the best memories, the experiences, the camaraderie, and the girlfriends. Whenever you bump into anyone who went there, you don't have to introduce yourself. But it's gone. I wish that all of you guys could have had a similar experience. Your brother, Josh, had it with the New England Music Camp.

Between the Bronx and Kinderwelt, I had a genuine foundation. It was insular, but somehow it was the beginning of having some confidence in myself. The normal fears of the future—college, the Army, and a vocation—were still formidable, but I was a little less afraid and therefore a little more adventurous.

3 THE GANG AND BLACKJACK KNEDLER

I went to PS 35 and then I went to Joseph H. Wade Junior High School. Lee Harvey Oswald, who shot Kennedy, went there. If you were smart you were RA "rapid advance" [Dad makes a "Ta Da!" noise] which meant that you skipped a half a grade or something like that. For high school, you had to take a test to get into Bronx Science, Stuyvesant, and Brooklyn Tech. Those were the big three. I don't know how—since I was not very good in science or math—but I got into Bronx Science.

When I went to high school, there were ten guys I hung out with. It was normal. We were like the pseudo-intellectual Bronx Science guys. We thought we were the chicest clique there could possibly be in the world and we thought it was exclusive. You know, we got together on the weekends, we went bowling together, and we went to parties together. What a delusion of self-importance! We thought we were the elite, and some of those guys *were* in many ways. We hung around together virtually every weekend. Proms, dances, bowling, and pinochle, and we pretended that we would all be friends for the rest of our lives but of course it was a youthful idea. We were very proud of "the gang."

We also went to the Broadway theatre. My first recollection of going to the theatre was when I was fourteen years old. I went to see a play called *Skipper Next to God*. It was with my Uncle Wolf Barzel, who was an actor, and he had a major role in the play. The play starred John Garfield, who in those days was a movie star from New York. I went backstage to meet him and on his dressing room door was a Jewish star—and above it was written "Julie" because that was his real name, Julie Garfinkel. That's my first recollection of going to the theatre. The heroes for us guys in the Bronx were people like Dane Clark, John Garfield, Richard Conte, all the same kind of New York Jewish and Italian street guys. They were all replaced by Marlon Brando in the fifties.

When I was seventeen, I saw Harry Belafonte and Gower Champion in *Three for Tonight*, and on one occasion we all took our dates to see Louis Calhern *in King Lear*. The actual truth was, when we saw Louis Calhern in *King Lear*, our opinion was totally pretentious—we didn't know what we were watching. We knew it was a great play, but we were bored.

I also saw *Death of a Salesman* and I walked out of the theatre as if I had been to the top of the mountain. *Death of a Salesman* is purportedly about the American Dream or the shattering of the American Dream, and about the relationship between fathers and sons. I think I was too young to know about the American Dream, but I remember thinking I had gone to some other place. The first time I saw the play, it was about fathers and sons, and it has remained so for the rest of my life. I never went to see *Death of a Salesman* again until Mike Nichols directed it with Philip Seymour Hoffman, and I had the same reaction as an adult as I did as a kid. Your mother and I walked out of the theatre in silence for four blocks.

That was maybe the seminal theatre experience and it's probably also why as a producer I did a lot of plays, not musicals. So the theatre was a part of my life and I guess it was embedded in me because when I was seventeen, the only medal I won at Bronx Science was the drama medal. As a kid, I saw a lot of shows, but the theatre was still a fantasy ambition—I wasn't brought up to aspire to those things.

At age fourteen or fifteen, I had no idea what my vocation was going to be. I knew I was not going to be a doctor, lawyer or engineer, none of which I was equipped to do. Bronx Science was filled with people who were brilliant. There was a kid, who at age sixteen, discovered that a paramecium, if it's not fertile enough, has a *ménage à trois*, and it was on the front page of *The New York Times*! The pluses were that you were exposed to some interesting and brilliant people. The negatives were that no matter what you did, there were twenty-three people who did it better, and so you thought that was the norm.

New York Times writer, Phil Shabecoff, who went to Bronx Science, wrote an article about this. He said when you think the norm is genius, then you are going to suffer from inferiority issues your whole life. That was partially true for me because the emphasis was on math and science, and I was less interested in that. My parents never pushed me to be anything, but there was one moment at age sixteen when the idea of being a doctor came up, and I cried because I didn't have an answer. I didn't want to be a doctor, I didn't want to be a lawyer, I didn't want to be anything. And that was Bronx Science.

Then I graduated and that was the end of it. The story of "the gang," Jews from the Bronx or Washington Heights whose parents were immigrants or first generation and what happened to them, is probably a very interesting story. About five of them became doctors, most of whom did not want to be doctors, but when you were twelve years old, you were told to be a doctor. That was the way out of the ghetto. In very many cases those are success stories in America but not fulfillment stories. A couple of guys who became doctors really wanted to do something else, but it was suppressed. I went to one reunion, a thirty-year Bronx Science reunion, and a guy who became a doctor came up to me and asked, "How'd you do it?"

He was referring to how I broke the mold of what the prescribed ambitions were. I didn't have an answer for him, but I did have an uncle who was an actor which meant that my sister and I went to see him perform. My uncle, Wolf Barzel, performed on Broadway a few times, which opened the door to another possibility for me. But in those days, I never thought of the theatre as a vocation because he struggled financially. I guess the best explanation is that a door opens. You either close the door or you walk through it to see what's on the other side, and one thing leads to another.

I then went to NYU Uptown in the Bronx. You dreamt about

going out of town, but you couldn't afford it. The cost of NYU was 750 dollars a year. My father paid it willingly because I didn't want to go to City College. I don't know why but he said, "Okay," and everything else I had to earn, so I worked as an usher at the Ritz Theatre.

NYU Uptown was a liberal arts and engineering school. It was all men and no women. It's now the Bronx Community College. My friend Harold Grossman, who had a car, would drive up from 104th Street and Lexington Avenue and pick me up. We'd drive up to the campus in University Heights. Since it was all men, there were no distractions. I participated in various things like the student council, and I was the president of the junior class. We went to dances—NYU invited women students from nursing schools and from Hunter College. You would go to the dance, and you'd say, "Hey, excuse me, would you like to dance?" You put on a jacket and a tie, and it was another kind of world.

I had a few really good teachers. I sort of knew it at the time, but it's only when you look back that you realize those teachers had an impact. The memorable teachers were Bill Vorenberg, James Welch, Professor McAdam, and Jack Knedler. These guys are not alive anymore, but they had a big influence on me. Bill Vorenberg was the head of the drama department. The speech and drama department was good. I went to audition for a play called *Death Takes a Holiday*. I got the part of "Death." Bill was very influential, and he loved the theatre, and everybody loved him. I found out later he really wasn't a very good director, but he was passionate about the theatre, and he inspired everybody. I really participated in that theatre group, and I loved it.

I remember I had a teacher in a course that I probably shouldn't have taken—constitutional law. He was a Scot, Professor McAdam, and he kept the windows open, so you'd freeze your ass off [Dad says in a Scottish accent]. You wouldn't fall asleep in that class because you were just too cold, but you got a sense of constitutional law. I should have paid more attention in that class.

I had a freshman English teacher, James Welch, who was about 6 foot 6 inches tall. He impressed us because with one hand he could move a desk that weighed a ton. He also taught at Fordham, conducted the chorale, and taught English at NYU. It wasn't any kind of course that I had ever taken. You had to write papers, the themes of which were arbitrary. A plane would fly overhead drowning out his lecture. He'd look up in the air and go, "Progress. That's your theme."

Then you'd write about progress from the "19th century to now" and he'd give you a C minus. I don't know what kind of exams we had, but I got a lot of C minuses. He'd write on the blackboard, and he couldn't erase the blackboard because it wasn't washed and he would say, "Blackboards that do not erase," and you'd write a paper on "Blackboards that do not erase." You didn't know what the hell you were doing. He didn't tell you what to write.

Then one day it snowed, and he said, "Snow, that's the theme," and I began to get an idea. I wrote a story about a man, and my image was Kinderwelt. It was about a man who lived in Kinderwelt, and he had to walk about a mile into Highland Mills to go to the funeral of his friend and it snowed. I got a B and then it dawned on me—he wanted you to write something out of your imagination. It's a year course and I wound up with a B, but that was a big lesson in my awareness.

I also took a Shakespeare course with a man named John Knedler. We called him "Blackjack Knedler." He was a Kittredge scholar of Shakespeare. I was told he was a part of Gertrude Stein's salon in Paris when he was young. He was obviously a gay man but there was no word for "gay" at that time. He was who he was, and he had stunning control of the English language. I was a somewhat pretentious English student. I ended up getting a B in the course, but I got a D plus on the first exam and he said, "Azenberg, you'll have a hard time in this course." [Dad says this in a deep voice.]

You didn't have a notebook and he didn't give you any theories about anything and he made you bring the full tome to the class. He just went through every tragedy, line by line, telling you the meaning of the words. I thought he was brilliant. He knew that we were babies. He said, "Don't make it complicated, just know what the play's about." You would write the meaning of the words in your tome. For example, in the *Hamlet* speech, he talks about "Thus conscience doth make cowards of us all," and John Knedler would ask, "What does conscience mean?"

Well, if you have a contemporary conversation about conscience, it would be about guilt, and you'd feel guilty and all of that. He'd say, "No, conscience just meant thinking– 'thus doth thinking make cowards of us all.' If you think about it too much, you don't do anything. If you don't know what these words mean, you don't know what the play means."

I asked him once why we couldn't take notes, and he said, "You'll throw the notes away. You'll never throw that book away."

He was correct because twenty years later, when I was working in the theatre and I had produced a few plays, your sister, Karen, was a student at NYU, and John Knedler retired. He had had a stroke and there was a dinner for him, and I was asked to go. I gave a speech and I said, "He was right. We didn't throw the book away because here it is," and I gave it to Karen. I said, "So there is some continuity." It justified the man's life. He didn't just teach and then the knowledge was gone or forgotten.

"Blackjack Knedler" was also on the student faculty discipline committee, which included all the deans, one arts college student and one engineering college student. There were 1250 arts students, 1250 engineering students, and I was the one student from the arts college who was a part of that committee. If you got caught plagiarizing, you had to appear before them. Even the deans of the college were intimidated by "Blackjack Knedler," due to his control of language.

There was a kid who was a freshman who wrote a paper on Iceland. Well, in 1953 there were maybe two books on Iceland in the world, and it was obvious that he had plagiarized them. He was terrified and Knedler came late to the meeting and then asked the kid, "Do you know the definition of plagiarism?"

The kid mumbled something or other. Knedler proceeded—without looking at a book—to give him the first definition, the second definition, whatever the dictionary said, and he asked, "If those are the definitions, did you plagiarize?"

Well, the kid is dead. He's up against the heavyweight champion. The kid said, "Yes."

And then Knedler, to show how understanding he was, said, "My suggestion is, we put a mark in your permanent record in pencil and if nothing comes up between now and your senior year, we erase it."

You know, many kids are going to go to graduate school, so to have a mark like that on their record would be devastating. That was the kind of guy he was. He was a great teacher.

What I enjoyed, I got good grades in, and I wound up with an eighty-seven average. It wasn't extraordinary and it wasn't a memorable college experience. I didn't have a lot of long-term friends that came out of college and I'm not sure why, but I've got to give NYU credit. I had several great professors. I think I was too young to be educated in a correct way, but they made the courses interesting, and they opened a door. I didn't walk through it then, but if they were alive today, I would thank them.

4 FOUR LIEUTENANTS AND A GENERAL

I got one D in college in my freshman semester... It was in ROTC, Reserve Officers' Training Corps... You know, marching around... I didn't care, but the irony is that I ultimately went into the ROTC. I wound up getting a D in the first semester, a C in the second semester, a B in the beginning of sophomore year, and an A at the end of sophomore second semester. Don't ask me what they were teaching us. I wore a military uniform for my entire four years in college. I didn't wear it every day, but I wore it three days a week. Then I had to decide during my sophomore year, which was in 1952, do I continue with the ROTC...?

I thought (correctly or arrogantly or for whatever the reason was) that I would continue. I thought going in as a lieutenant was better than going in as a private. The Korean War was on, and the story was that the lieutenants got killed first, but I said I'm gonna do it anyway. Mind you, everybody knew that they were gonna go into the service. You were either drafted or you joined, so I joined. I also knew that because I was an English major, there was no military priority. They could take you right out of school, but if you went into the ROTC, they let you finish your education. You then went wherever they wanted you to go.

When you were young and growing up in the Bronx your mother would ask, "What are you going to do? When are you getting married?"

Those were the two big questions. If you were going into the service, they didn't ask you those questions because you had to get through it. I made the decision to continue with the ROTC and it turned out to be a sensationally good decision. One, the Korean War ended in my junior year. And two, my experience in the Army was a really good one—I ended up achieving the rank of cadet captain.

In my junior year at NYU, they sent me to Fort Meade in Maryland for boot camp, and for six weeks they beat the hell out of you. There were some funny stories because New Yorkers going for the first time into a real disciplined place is hysterical. You learned to polish your boots, to clean your rifle, to shoot weapons, to read maps, to make your bed perfectly, and you got on your hands and knees to pick up every speck of dust. The sergeants and officers were yelling at you. They didn't let up on you at all.

When you finished, the same guys that were driving you crazy, came over and shook your hand because you got through it. You found out what basic training was. When you graduated college, you went to the graduation ceremony in your military uniform. At the graduation ceremony, they pinned the lieutenant's bars on your shoulder. I forget who it was who pinned it, maybe my mother or my father, but I was now a lieutenant in the United States Army.

So, I graduated from NYU in June and because my date to go into active duty wasn't until October or November, I did summer stock as an actor at The Peninsula Players in Fish Creek, Wisconsin. I got 15 dollars a week and room and board. I did plays like *The Caine Mutiny Court Martial.* I was in four or five plays as an actor. *The Rainmaker*, they made a movie and a musical out of that; *110 in the Shade* and *Sabrina... The Moon's Blue?...* I don't know, something like that. When I came home from Wisconsin, I knew I couldn't just hang around, so I got a job at Gimbels as a floorwalker. I lied to them because I knew I wasn't going to stay there long.

Then it was time to put on my uniform. It was the first adventurous choice I made. "I don't want to do this, I don't want to do that," is the normal thing, but I said, "Yes, I'm gonna go." I don't think my father had any objection to it and I don't think he even understood it, but what he did understand (and my mother understood as well) was that everyone was expected to go into the service. If you were a doctor, you could go in as a doctor, or if you had a particular ability—like being an engineer—then you would do that. There was a certain pride in being an infantry officer. When I say that to contemporary people, they look at me like I came from somewhere else. That decision allowed me to finish school. The Korean War ended and then I went into the Army between Korea and Vietnam. If I did it in another way, I might not be here and [speaking to me] you might be somebody else.

Then I left for Fort Benning in Georgia. I flew down to Atlanta and took a train from Atlanta to Columbus. In the first six weeks that you're there, you know nobody and you're just in a new place. I thought if I could get out of there, I would get out of there. I got to Fort Benning at the beginning of November and six weeks later there was the Christmas break. I went back up to New York and had a week at home.

When I came back to Fort Benning it was okay. Everything was okay. The training was not as brutal as the Fort Meade training. It was called Basic Infantry Officer's Course—BIOC #7. There were two hundred of us, from all over America. It was my first time out of the city, and I was in another world where I met people from Kentucky, Texas, and Oklahoma and I got to see the South a little bit. It's where I met Bill Hogarty and Dave McCullough. Bill, Dave, and I became good friends. McCullough played basketball for UC Santa Barbara. Bill Hogarty was a devout Catholic and was an all-American baseball player and soccer player. We were all friendly at Fort Benning, but we didn't become really friendly until we shipped out to Schofield Barracks in Hawaii.

In any case, the training was interesting... and it was for strange purposes. You learned how to kill people. The leadership school was spectacular. Leadership school is where they put you through some tests so that you make decisions right away because you're not going to get any more information. You don't say, "But yeah let me find out if...." No no no, bang! Because that's the way it is on the battlefield evidently. Maybe the totality is that we were the luckiest people in the United States because we all joined during the Korean War, and they didn't put us on active duty until after the Korean War ended. All of us were in the infantry, which are the ground troops, and we weren't very sophisticated. We expected to go to Korea and many who came after us went to Vietnam. When we finished at Fort Benning, a great camaraderie had developed amongst all of us.

Then we got the orders that we weren't going to Korea. One hundred and seventy guys went to Europe, and thirty (including Hogarty, McCullough, and I) went to Hawaii—United States Army Pacific. We were posted at Schofield Barracks on the island of Oahu. There was a party to celebrate that we weren't going to Korea. Of the two hundred men, one hundred of them were married. These men were twenty-two and twenty-three years old. If you went to Korea, you didn't bring your wife. If you went to the Pacific or Europe, you brought your wife and household goods. The Army shipped them for you—your car, your wife, your children—so there was some celebration. There was a party, but I don't remember much. It was maybe one of the few times in my life that I was drunk, because I don't really like to drink. I only remember somebody pouring something on my head and I was standing on top of a pool table.

When I arrived at Schofield Barracks, I met another guy named Tom Anderson who was originally from Ohio or maybe Kentucky. He played football for Miami University in Ohio, and he was a big strong man. Tom Anderson, Bill Hogarty, Dave McCullough, and I became great friends. It's a whole part of your life that balances you. It gives you yet another experience and yeah... it's maybe an innocent time, a youthful time, but I have images of all of us wearing American military uniform, walking, shooting the breeze, laughing. Tom was married to his wife Carol when we were out there, and on Sunday afternoons, Hogarty and I spent time with the Anderson family. McCullough got married when he found out we weren't going to Korea. We left him alone on weekends.

It was my first experience outside of my own neighborhood. I'm in a company of two hundred men, and there are only four or five Jews, and the fact that it didn't matter was an interesting experience. I always expected antisemitic stuff because the books that we read indicated that there would be all sorts of incidents. You always had your name either on your helmet or on your name tag—so they can see that your name is "Azenberg" and right away they know. I was always conscious of that, but McCullough, Hogarty, Anderson, and I stayed friends and in touch with each other for our whole lives. We didn't have so much in common personally, except that these were good people, and we shared a camaraderie.

There are lots of anecdotes that we can talk about, but just so you have it for the record, Father Rusnock was a captain and the chaplain for the 14th Infantry. He was a cigar-smoking, foxhole guy. He ultimately left the Church and married a nun, by the way. Father Rusnock spread the word that any time he gave an Old Testament sermon, Lieutenant Azenberg wrote it, which was totally untrue. It was his effort to suppress any prejudices.

So, it's Mother's Day and Hogarty throws my bed over and he says, "We're going to church today!"

I remember saying to him, "Saturday! Saturday!" and pointing to myself, "*Jews*, Saturday! *You*, Sunday!"

He just said, "Come on! We're going!"

When you go to church, you put on a first-class uniform, it's respect. We drive up to the church and the officers are supposed to sit in the front pews and the enlisted men sit in the back. I don't want to sit in the front, so I say, "Bill, let's sit in the back."

He says, "No no no, officers in the front."

There are not too many people in the church and we're in the first pew. Opposite us, across the aisle, is General McGee. He is a one-star general who was a hero in World War II and the Korean War and he's a good Catholic. He glances over and he sees the Jewish lieutenant in the first pew. When he looks at me, I nod my head because I know how to genuflect with the best of them. Genuflecting, you know what that is? [Speaking to me.] I knew when you go down, when you go up, and all of that.

Father Rusnock comes out in his full outfit. He's not in his uniform, he's wearing his priestly vestments and he winks at me, with General McGee watching this. Father Rusnock proceeds to give a sermon about Mary (because it's Mother's Day) and concludes with, "Mary achieved the fulfillment of every Jewish maiden," and Father Rusnock winks at me again. General McGee watches this.

When the Mass is over, Father Rusnock walks down the aisle, then the ranking officers go, then the lieutenants go. By the time Hogarty and I get out of the church, General McGee is standing next to Father Rusnock. We walk by and salute the General and say, "Good morning, sir."

Father Rusnock asks, "Wasn't Azenberg's sermon good?"

It was totally untrue. I had nothing to do with it.

A month or so later, Colonel Surles and Colonel Kelly arrived at the 25th Infantry. Each of them had a good-looking daughter, and Hogarty and I wanted to invite the daughters to attend various military functions and dances. There's no messing around—you don't want to get killed by their fathers. And remember we were not career officers, so these two colonels didn't know who we were. On top of that, they are Protestant, Hogarty is a Catholic, and I'm Jewish, so that's screwing everything up.

They called General McGee and asked, "General, who are these two lieutenants that want to take out our daughters?"

General McGee evidently said, "You should be honored."

When I tell you these anecdotes about my days in the Army with the 25th Infantry, 94% of our time was getting up at five o'clock in the morning when they taught us jungle training and military exercises. So if you take some of these moments out of context, you might think we went to summer camp. But no, it wasn't that at all. This was a crack unit, and we were all committed soldiers. The 25th is an historic American unit and there was an intimacy amongst us. It was in the fifties, and the Jewish kid and the Catholic kid were thrown together. It wasn't unique but I think, at least for that moment, it overcame the prejudices of the time. McCullough, Hogarty, Anderson, and I were really good friends. We were twenty-three or twenty-four-year-old unsophisticated young men and things were much simpler then. It was a very seminal part of my life.

When Hogarty left the Army, he came back to the States, played AA baseball and then broke his leg, and had to retire. He did all sorts of other things to make a living. He remained a devout Catholic his whole life. The priests called him "the bishop" because he was a better man than those who were committed to it. Hogarty married a girl from Boston, and he and his wife eventually moved back to

Hawaii.

Did I tell you the story of Bill Hogarty coming over for the first time to meet my father? Ya know, my father was an intelligent man and Bill was this devout Catholic. I mean, a *devout* Catholic, and most things were related to the Good Lord. I remember my mother made hamburgers, which we hadn't had in a while. So we were eating, and my father asked Bill, "Bill, you talk to God? I mean literally?"

Hogarty said, "Yeah."

Well, that really got to my father.

There was a long pause and then he asked Bill, "Does he talk back to you?"

Hogarty said, "Yeah."

It was unheard of. There's this normal American well-spoken athlete who talks to God, and God talks back.

McCullough became a Superintendent of Schools in the Santa Ynez Valley in California where Reagan had his ranch. McCullough was a Democrat, but he kept that job because he was a real educator. Tom stayed in the military and retired as a lieutenant colonel. He fought in two wars, Vietnam and Korea, and managed to survive. At first, he was gung-ho about the Vietnam War but when he came back two years later he simply said, "We don't belong there. It's corrupt." And he blamed the politicians and he retired from the service.

At one point, the Hogarty family and the Anderson family wanted to move to Hawaii, but they didn't have any money. The Hogarty family was living in Massachusetts and the Anderson family was living in Ohio. I had just had my first success on Broadway—it was probably *Ain't Misbehavin'*—so I lent them the money.

The truth is, you never want to lend anybody money, but these were friends and there was no way to say no. I gave them one check for 10,000 dollars and one check for 8,000 dollars, and they moved to Hawaii. One year later, Tom Anderson sat down on a couch and died. They found he had a hole in his heart. This man survived two wars and twenty years in the military, and then sat down on a couch and died. He was teaching junior high school at the time.

Hogarty stayed in Hawaii for seventeen years but was eventually diagnosed with cancer and was going to die. I flew out to Hawaii, and I spent five days with him to say goodbye. He was living in Maui, and I remember we sat on a beach that overlooked Oahu. We spoke about how time flew, and we pictured the two of us wandering around Schofield Barracks together. I remember thinking that fifty years ago we were all young men. Then we hugged and said goodbye, and six months later he died.

Shortly afterward, both the Anderson and Hogarty families sold their houses in Hawaii and moved back to the States. I then received two checks in the mail within three or four months of each other—one check for 10,000 dollars and one for 8,000 dollars. Nobody had said a word about it in that whole period. I didn't ask for it and in truth, I really forgot about it, but they didn't. When I received the checks, I didn't know whether I should cash them or not. I felt a little guilty in a strange way, but I did eventually cash them.

I loved those guys. You must work at maintaining the important friendships that you make in your life. The transiency of relationships is scary to me. The distancing that can happen between children and parents, or friends, is something we've all experienced. The fact that I was now in my late forties, and we still had this connection was a good feeling. The camaraderie that I had with them has been hard to come by in my life because I think relationships in the theatre are so much more transient.

I'm not sure what we all had in common, but our mutual experience in the service lasted, and I feel it to this day. I miss them. I miss talking to them and I miss seeing them. I don't think I could spend my whole day with them because we're now involved in different worlds. But in some theoretical or romantic way, if I were in trouble, I think the plane would land and those guys would get off the plane and bail me out. I'm not sure that there are many people in my current vocation who I can rely on in the same way. I really liked those guys. It wasn't about showbusiness, it wasn't about education, it wasn't about anything. It was about camaraderie.

When I joined the 14th Infantry, Colonel Ferguson was my first regimental commander. He was a West Pointer and a career military man. About a year later, Colonel Ferguson was transferred to Fort Ord in California. It is very unusual for a rinky-dink lieutenant, who is not a career officer, to stay in touch with a colonel throughout their entire lives, but we did.

I think he liked me. I think he liked that I was a loyal member of the regiment. He was the one that promoted me from second lieutenant to first lieutenant. I thought he was a good and dedicated man without prejudice. Hogarty and I were great examples of that unit—we were the Catholic kid and the Jewish kid. He didn't abide prejudice towards anyone, including the two Black officers in the regiment. Remember this was in 1955 or 1956, and because of that, everybody behaved—we didn't screw around.

Colonel Ferguson married a woman whose father was also the regimental commander of the 14th infantry. They had a son named Bobby, who was sixteen years old when we were at Schofield Barracks. Bobby got killed in Vietnam calling in artillery fire on his own position, which was overrun by the Viet Cong. This devastated the old man. There was also a lieutenant with me in the first battalion named Frank Wells, who later became president of Disney. Ferguson, who became a major general, kept in touch with both of us for forty years and he was proud of his two lieutenants who became surrogate sons.

Rebecca, your sister, was born on the 14th of February. The general said, "She's a daughter of the regiment." And he sent Rebecca a shirt that said, "U.S. Military Academy 14th Infantry—Ferguson."

So I said to General Ferguson, "There's a strange continuity in life in ways we would not have anticipated."

General Ferguson retired to Pebble Beach, and when we had shows in San Francisco, he would always be invited. When he needed tickets, he could get them, anywhere and for anybody. We always made sure that he was taken care of.

Years later, when the general was fading, I drove down to Pebble Beach to have lunch with him, and his wife said to me, "He barely gets out of bed anymore, but for you he'll get fully dressed."

General Ferguson died right after 9/11 and the burial took

place at West Point. Your mother and I drove up and there were only twelve people at the funeral. Three four-star generals, one of whom was General Westmoreland, head of the Army in Vietnam and the former Commandant of West Point—he graduated from West Point with General Ferguson.

I was only a lieutenant and General Ferguson's wife said, "I knew you'd be here."

General Westmoreland looked at your mother and said, "You have beautiful legs."

I thought he was a little nuts.

When we went to the funeral ceremony, they presented the flag to the widow. They fired rifles and they played taps through the valley... West Point, it's a beautiful place. Then General Westmoreland walked over to the coffin and just saluted the coffin and said farewell to a comrade. It was very moving.

Remember, when I was in the Army I was in my early twenties. It was a huge experience to meet people from all over the United States. I really didn't experience antisemitism—with one exception. When I first joined the 14th infantry, my first company commander said, "Well, we had a Jew in our outfit once. He wasn't much but we'll see what you are." [Dad imitates him in a stern Southern accent.]

That was the only incident. And meeting all these people... Interesting... And this is, ya know, a long time before I met your mother.

5 A BEGINNING

When you grew up in the neighborhood that I grew up in at that time, you didn't date non-Jewish girls. This wasn't just limited to the Jews. The Italians married the Italians, the Irish married the Irish... We didn't know what a Protestant was. I dated Ellie at Kinderwelt. We met in camp, and she was a freshman or sophomore in college, and I was a sophomore or junior in college and we went out in the summer. She worked in the office, and I was a counselor, and then we broke up. She lived in Massachusetts, and I was in New York, so I mean, ya know... But while I was in the Army, I dated a little. Not a lot, but a little.

Dave McCullough was the coach of the United States Army Pacific Basketball Team, and I was the officer in charge. The team traveled to Fort Monmouth, New Jersey, which is close to New York, and I arranged to see Ellie—I hadn't seen a nice Jewish girl in the Pacific. We wound up going out and she looked very attractive, and we necked for a week. Then I went back to Schofield Barracks, and during that time Ellie and I corresponded, and a year later I came out of the Army.

When I came home, Ellie was going out with Arnie Schwartz, whom I went to school with. He was a friend of mine. So now it's a competition. I won the competition and I probably exhausted myself because I was twenty-five years old, and Ellie and I ended up getting engaged.

Before I went into the Army, I thought about acting as a career—it was glamorous, different, and frightening. When I came out of the Army, I was older and the idea of walking around town with my picture and resumé went right out the window. It was not a difficult decision to make because of the fear that I had of not being able to make a living. I never thought of the theatre as a place where you made a living. It's sort of an avocation rather than a vocation. I was fortunate that I made that decision early. It was never an extended suppressed desire and it only lasted for a few minutes. I jokingly say I found out what work was like in the Army, and I knew I didn't want to do that, but I thought I could work doing something in the theatre.

When I came out of the Army, there were places I could not live and there were jobs I could not have because I was Jewish. The theatre was one place that had no restrictions. For the most part, the entertainment business in America, both on Broadway and in Hollywood, did not have restrictions. I was looking for a job in a world that I knew nothing about. Louis Perkiss, a friend of my parents, married Max Segal's daughter. Max Segal was a Broadway general manager and somehow, through all of that, I got a job in management or production or whatever words one used at that time. I got a job working for a theatre agent—Briscoe, Goldsmith, and Arthur—and in their heyday they were the agents for the Lunts and many other stars. They had a small office on 5th Avenue.

I'm the 50-dollar-a-week gofer. I do everything. After being a first lieutenant in the Army and leading a platoon, it's a bit of a comedown, but I work there for a year. I meet a few people and I do the books. I do anything and everything. Nothing was that complicated. There were no computers in those days. Hartney Arthur, who was Australian, was revitalizing the agency a little bit because it's an old-line agency and he's going to produce *The Legend of Lizzie* on Broadway. Stuart Vaughn, who was a director at the New York Shakespeare Festival, is going to direct it. I get 60 dollars a week.

At some point Ellie and I get married, and she is probably making 80 dollars a week working at Bonwit Teller which is a chic store. I am the assistant company manager and Bernie Gersten, who later ran the New York Shakespeare Festival/The Public Theater for Joe Papp and Lincoln Center Theater, was the stage manager. It had a wonderful cast, but it was a terrible production. Stuart Vaughn quits or gets fired, Hartney Arthur takes over and makes it more terrible. It ran four performances, and it was gone. It played at the 54th St Theatre. There is no 54th St Theatre anymore, but I discover that I can do a company manager's job.

I'm now out of work. I go back to the Bronx, and I get a job with Mel Halpern, a guy I went to school with. His father runs a liquor store in the Bronx, and I deliver liquor crates for 55 dollars under the table each week. Then I get a job for the summer as the company manager for the Rye Music Circus in Rye, New York. The general manager of the Rye Music Circus was Roy Somlyo and we got along.

I am getting 75 dollars a week, and I have a room up in Rye, and at this point Ellie is pregnant with Karen. It's part of the St. John Terrell summer stock touring circuit. In those days there were two summer stock touring circuits—Guber, Ford & Gross and St. John Terrell. Summer stock musicals were performed in tents and there were six permanent tents around the East Coast. Each show would start in a tent and play for a week or two, then that show would leave to perform in another tent, and a new show would come in.

That summer, the program was *The Merry Widow, Bells are Ringing, Brigadoon, Du Barry Was a Lady,* and *Ziegfeld Follies of 19*-something or other. Those shows starred Doretta Morrow, Jack Washburn, Bert Wheeler, and Bert Lahr. *The Merry Widow* was my first exposure to musicals, and this was in an era when there were no microphones, so the singers really sang these songs and they all had big voices, so it was exciting.

The Merry Widow was not successful because it originated in 1910 and it had been performed too many times, but it was exciting for me. I grew up with plays and there was something theoretically about musicals that made no sense to me—people didn't stop and sing in my world, in the Bronx. *The Merry Widow* was silly, but I loved the music. The music that I like today, both classical and contemporary, is melodious. The Franz Lehár score in *The Merry Widow* is so melodic and there was also something exciting about seeing an audience's reaction when it was good. I also listened to the score of *Brigadoon* probably at every performance. It was sung by people with extraordinarily good voices. This was during the romantic Broadway period.

For the life of me, I couldn't tell you what *Du Barry Was a Lady* was about, but it starred Bert Lahr, the Cowardly Lion from *The Wizard of Oz*. He was a comedian, a star, genuinely funny, and the audience loved him. The stage lights were hung in the middle of the tent, and they would attract moths at night. Bert Lahr hated the moths because they were disrupting his performance—ya know, they'd fly over here and over there. But all you have to know about Bert Lahr is that if there's a problem one night, the next night he would deal with it. It was the 4th of July, and in the middle of the show, fireworks were set off nearby and no one could hear the performance. I don't know how he did it, but when the fireworks started, Bert Lahr stopped the show and began to direct traffic with the moths! One moth would fly here, and another moth would fly there, and he does a whole routine and the audience falls down laughing.

The last show of the season, *The Ziegfeld Follies of 19*-something or other, was a variety show with Bert Wheeler, who was a Vaudeville star. After performing the show in Lambertville, New Jersey, we moved to the Rye Music Circus. The previous manager at the Rye Music Circus had not paid the bills to the manager in Lambertville, so none of the scenery, props, or music for our show was going to be delivered to us. Roy Somlyo asked me if I could drive a truck. I had never driven a truck. I said, "Not a semi."

He said, "No, you know, a twenty-foot truck."

I said, "I can drive but it'll be..."

Roy used to be the general manager at Lambertville, so he knew where everything was stored. At midnight on Saturday or Sunday we left Rye, and we drove a couple of hours in a truck to Lambertville. We stole everything and loaded up the truck. We got back at about five o' clock in the morning and we did the show that night.

About fifty years later, Roy got an award, and I was asked to speak. I remember saying, "It's very nice that Roy is getting this award, but I think that the committee should know that both he and

I are felons, and that this award is being presented to a man who is a thief and who has not been prosecuted to this day."

That summer I got paid 75 dollars a week and I worked seven days a week, and I loved it. Those were some of the shows I did, and it was a beginning, and I began to meet people.

The summer was over and I was out of work, but I was recommended by Roy Somlyo to be the company manager for an off-Broadway show at the Renata Theatre down on MacDougal Street. That show was *Lend an Ear*, a musical originally done on Broadway by Gower Champion, in which Carol Channing was discovered. It's being produced by a guy named Stephen Slade, who ran one of the summer tents on the north shore near Boston. I have a nineteen-year-old assistant but I'm doing all the work. This is now real. Charles Nelson Reilly is also in the cast, and he is not good, he's superb. The show also had Jenny Lou Law, Elizabeth Allen, Al Checco, and all of these first-rate actors. It was thrilling. I could watch it almost every night. Walter Kerr of *The Herald Tribune* gave it a rave notice, but *The New York Times* only gave it a mixed review. I watched the show a lot because it was the closest thing to a Broadway experience that I had been involved with.

One night, for a very limited audience at midnight, the cast decided to do the entire show where the men played the women, and the women played the men. My recollection is that I never laughed so hard in my life, and I realized how good these performers were. The show ran eleven weeks and then it closed. Charlie Reilly and I remained friends because we shared a mutual experience. He did twenty off-Broadway shows before he made his Broadway debut and then he became a big star, but in the industry, everybody knew who he was.

The next show at the Renata Theatre was called *Sappho* and it was a play about homosexuality. It only ran about two weeks, and it wasn't very good, but I'm in showbusiness now. I have two shows on my resumé, I've done summer stock, and I've entered the showbusiness world.

At that time, which is around 1960, there is a union job on every Broadway show called "a company manager." The union is the Association of Theatrical Press Agents & Managers (ATPAM), and it is what was called a closed shop. I think it's somewhat of a contradiction that the managers had a union, but you couldn't work on Broadway unless you were a member of ATPAM. You couldn't get into the union unless you were selected, and it was very difficult to get in. The head of that union was Milton Weintraube, who was a friend of my Uncle Wolfie. I told Weintraube that I would love to get into the union and he asked, "What are you working on now?"

I said, "I'm working on a show off Broadway for 75 dollars a week."

He said, "Well, we are going to try and organize off Broadway so you would have to leave your job."

I remember saying, "I have a wife and child. I am responsible for feeding them. Who is going to take care of them if not me?"

He very gruffly said, "Well, we don't really care about that and if you want to get into this union, you'll do what I say."

I took his desk, threw it over, and said some unpleasant words about him and his union. I was insulted. When I walked in there, I was in showbusiness. And when I walked out, I was out of showbusiness.

I applied for a job at CBS as a clerk. I got the job, and it was one step above an entry level job. Then I moved up to 108 dollars a week in the operations department and I worked 9am to 5pm or 10am to 6pm, whatever it was. I am in charge of scheduling assistant directors and stage managers, one of whom is Joe Papp, who goes on to start the New York Shakespeare Festival/The Public Theater.

There was a threatened strike (I forget by whom) and the CBS operations department had to prepare for what they would do in case of such a strike. It was our department's job to figure out which assistant directors and stage managers covered which shows, so I laid out a schedule. I didn't think it was that complicated. I figured out that a guy who used to be a production assistant and who used to be an assistant director, could cover whatever show, and I organized it. There were some very bright people in that group. My job at CBS was a good job and it probably had a future.

I was there for about six or seven months, when Roy Somlyo called up and said, "I'm working now as a general manager for Alex Cohen [who was a big-time Broadway producer]. We're going to be running the summer program at the O'Keefe Center in Toronto, which is a brand-new glorious building. Would you like to be the company manager?"

I asked, "How much?"

He said, "150 dollars while you're in New York, and 225 dollars plus a hotel in Toronto. You'll get a nice set of rooms, so you can bring your wife and child."

So I got a leave of absence from CBS because I did a good job on the potential strike, and I started working for Alex Cohen.

I remember getting 150 dollars which netted down to about 121 dollars and for that I would go wherever they told me. At that time, Ellie and I were living at 35 West 92nd Street. I came home that day, and I literally threw the money up in the air. This was a union job, but Washington had just passed the Taft-Hartley Act and it ended the closed shop. I could now be hired because the union cannot prevent a man from working. If I am offered work, ATPAM has to make a decision whether they take me into the union or not, but they cannot prevent me from working. I am obligated to then apply to the union, and they can take me or not. They don't take me, but I am doing a company manager's job.

I went up to Toronto for the summer where I got paid 225 dollars and we did *West Side Story*. It was directed by Ruthie Mitchell, Hal Prince's Broadway stage manager, and choreographed by Tommy Abbott, who was Jerome Robbins' assistant. We did a crackerjack production of *West Side Story* and it sold out. The top ticket price was $3.50, the 3,000-seat place sells out for two weeks, and we do a one-week return engagement.

In between those two productions of *West Side Story,* there was Peter, Paul and Mary, Vic Damone, and Eartha Kitt, and all sorts of stars doing one-weekers. It was genuinely exciting working with all of these people, and Eartha Kitt wanted to know if I'd be her manager. Roy asked if I wanted to come back next year because this was a successful summer, so I said, "Sure."

I go back to CBS, expecting to be given a better job. They give me a job, but it's the job of scheduling the trucks. And that's it. That's the end of my CBS career. I am smitten with the theatre.

I'm in Alex Cohen's office to manage a tour of a number of cities with Lena Horne. It's what Alex Cohen called his *Nine o' Clock Revue* show. There would be various variety stars, like Nichols and May and The Delta Rhythm Boys. So I go out on tour with Lena Horne and Don Adams, who later went on to do *Get Smart*. It was a great learning experience.

The highlight of the evening was Lena Horne, who was beautiful, and every night the audience wanted her to sing "Stormy Weather," but she never sang it. They would bring her out, encore after encore, but still no "Stormy Weather." The audience now knows she's not going to sing it, and they begin to leave. Her husband, Lenny Hayton, was the conductor of the orchestra. I don't know how they timed it, but there would be twenty people in the aisle ready to leave and then in acapella you'd hear Lena sing, "Don't know why..." [Dad sings...] and you'd see people freeze. People sat down in their seats... "There's no sun up in the sky.... stormy weather..." [Dad sings again] And the place erupted. She did this at every performance.

I also did a Rodgers and Hammerstein revue with Barbara Cook, Earl Wrightson, Anita Darian, and Bill Tabbert. It's a one-week show with eight performances of Rodgers and Hammerstein music and the opening night would be conducted by Richard Rodgers. Bill Tabbert sang "Younger Than Springtime," Earl Wrightson sang, "Soliloquy," Anita Darian sang "You'll Never Walk Alone," and Barbara Cook sang "Shall We Dance."

Barbara Cook did not really want to sing "Shall We Dance," which was originally written for Gertrude Lawrence, who did not have a great vocal range. She did not want to sing the song at its normal fast pace [Dad sings the song and I, of course, sing along]. She wanted to sing it as a ballad. Nobody had ever heard that song sung in that way. "We've... just... been... introduced...." [Dad sings it very slowly]. She sings it in that gorgeous voice that she had. "Shall.... we...dance...." Well, she needed Rodgers' permission in order to sing it that way. He came in that Monday afternoon and said, "Okay, let me hear it."

Barbara Cook was the most gorgeous singer anywhere and she sang "Shall We Dance" as a ballad for Richard Rodgers and it was simply breathtaking. Rodgers nodded his head and said, "Okay."

Rodgers conducted the opening night and Barbara Cook stopped the show. It was a beautiful success. The next day, I was in the office in Toronto on the phone with my wife Ellie, suggesting she fly up to see the show because it was so terrific. Barbara Cook and Bill Tabbert walked by the office and Tabbert asked, "Who are you talking to?"

I said, "I'm talking to my wife."

He said, "Wait a minute."

He called Barbara Cook over and they sang a duet on the phone to Ellie. Tabbert and I remained friends. I also remained friends with Barbara Cook and later I produced her show *Barbara Cook on Broadway*. Your mother and I went up to The Carlisle whenever she was singing. She was legendary.

I did the last show of the season in Toronto in 1963 with Phyllis Diller. She did the first half of the show and then there was an ice show. It was a 3,000-seat theatre and it grossed about 8,000 dollars for the week, which meant that nobody showed up. It was a disaster. The O'Keefe Center was pretty new and in order to do an ice show.... you think Canada and an ice show.... ya know, well, we didn't quite make the ice. You have to make ice by electricity, and it took a while because it was the summer, so it was more of a slush show. The skaters didn't go quite as fast on slush in the opening number as they should have. It was a disaster.

On the take-out, the last of the season, they had covered the deck with Celotex so that any melted water wouldn't leak onto the wooden deck. They picked up the Celotex at about three o'clock in the morning and there's a puddle of water.

The carpenter said to the property man, "Ollie, go mop up this water..."

And the property man at three o'clock in the morning said, "No no no, that's not property water, that's electric water. It's not my jurisdiction." The property man explained that this water came from the ice, and the ice was manufactured by electricity from Niagara Falls. This was not property water; this was electric water.

The electrician's name was Miller, and he said, "I'm not mopping that up. It's certainly not electric water, it's not my jurisdiction."

So the property man wouldn't mop it up, and the electrician wouldn't mop it up, and the carpenter's deck is getting wet.

The carpenter was a guy named Grant Milligan. He went over and picked up Ollie by his neck and said, "Mop up this water!"

This was my first union jurisdictional dispute at three o' clock in the morning. There would be many more, and the carpenter was correct.

Alex Cohen was a showman, and he was hustling the O'Keefe Center. He would over-inflate the costs and I knew it. I didn't know the specifics, but the shows cost, let's say 30,000 dollars, and Alex told them they cost 40,000 dollars. He kept the difference and they found out.

The O'Keefe Center called me in to talk one day and I knew it was a pump job. The people in Canada were trusting and honorable people and they were being cheated. In any case, it was a disastrous ending and I remember almost shaking while I was driving back to New York. That virtually ended my career with Alex, and I never worked for him again. He was a great showman with some serious flaws. He cheated. How can you do that? It's one thing to be a tough negotiator, but cheating your own group, your partners... It's straight out hustling your own.

Regardless, I'm now beginning to play a little bit more in the big leagues.

6 THE MERRICK OFFICE

I got back to New York, and I saw every show possible. I usually knew the company manager, so I rarely paid. I then got an offer from David Merrick's office. I had been bothering the Merrick office for a while because they had the most work. One of my first shows at the Merrick office was with Barbra Streisand in *I Can Get It for You Wholesale* in New York, which I had only a little to do with. The show was running in New York, and I eventually became the company manager. Nobody knew at that time that Barbra Streisand could sing because the song she sang in *I Can Get It for You Wholesale* was a patter song, which had a four-note range. One night the people in the office went down to one of those clubs in the village where young people would sing late at night. Well, Barbra opened her mouth, and everybody went, "Holy Mackerel!!"

I was going to go out on the road with the touring company which starred Larry Kert. The other original lady in it... they made a movie about her life... *I'll Cry Tomorrow*. She was a drunk. She drank and then she stopped drinking. She beat it in the end... Lillian Roth.

My first stop on the road was in Pittsburgh. I come back from that, and I tell the general manager Jack Schlissel, "I'll never get this. This is too complicated."

He looked at me and said, "Yes you will. Get the fuck out of here."

I went back to Pittsburgh, and he was right. It was kind of a second-rate tour. It was not a great show, but Larry Kert was a great guy—I mean, a really great guy. We got along and we were friends. He was also a stuntman, and he could do a pratfall... Ya know, like kick the back of your heel, and fly through the air and then splat. He would do it at hotels. One time in Baltimore, he went through the revolving door of the hotel and took a fall. It looked like he'd died, and he would do it just to upgrade his room. Management would come and there's the star of the show lying on the hotel floor. What can we do?! We'll give him a better room! Then Larry would get a suite. We remained kind of friendly on and off, and he eventually died of AIDS. [Speaking to me] Your mother and I went to the last show that he gave with Carol Lawrence at The Top of the Rock... Yeah, that was sad...

We also played the Fisher Theatre in Detroit, which is where I first met D.T. Nederlander. D.T. Nederlander was a tyrant. He's firing the house engineer for giving the previous show the correct kilowatt hours. That's how you paid for the electricity for your show. You came in, you read the meter, and if it said 10 kilowatts and when you left it said 20 kilowatts, you paid for 10 kilowatts. But D.T. always wanted to increase the kilowatt hours a little bit more so he could make a profit.

This poor guy is crying because he's been fired for being honest. Meanwhile Jimmy Nederlander Sr. is begging his father not to do this, and Joey Nederlander is re-hiring him in the other room. I thought that I would go back into the Army because these people were crazy! Anyhow, I am now becoming knowledgeable and I'm actually doing a good job. I'm paying attention to details, and I love the camaraderie.

I ultimately come back to New York after *I Can Get It for You Wholesale*. I've paid my dues. I'm now getting paid a salary. For the most part I'm working at the Merrick office on a regular basis. I think one of the first shows that I did for him in New York was *The Rehearsal*, a play by the famous French playwright Jean Anouilh. It was a play that Merrick was importing from London, starring Alan Badel, Keith Michell, Adrienne Corri, Jennifer Hilary and... I forgot the name of.... I'll give you the name of the woman who was the star... she was like one of these grand ladies... Coral Browne. Coral Browne was like the legendary Maggie Smith of her time. She could cut you dead with her words. Anouilh's plays were what we used to call "Boulevard plays."

Ironically, if you look at the totality of what I produced or managed, I must have worked on three or four of those types of plays, including *Rendezvous de Senlis,* which I later produced off Broadway. It is significant only in the fact that the "Boulevard" plays are like Neil Simon's plays except they're French—Neil Simon was accused of being a "Boulevard" playwright. When I think about it, it is something that I genuinely enjoyed in the theatre aesthetically. The language and the whimsical ideas that are not a joke, but humorous.

While I'm working on that, I'm also preparing a play called *Luther* to go on the road. Albert Finney is a new star who is coming from England to play *Luther* on Broadway. He's a good guy and we all go out drinking together. I'm working on lots of different shows for reasons that ATPAM, which I'm still not a member of, would not approve of. I did a lot of work, and I was getting paid.

At some point Jack Schlissel sent me out on the road with *Oliver!* The critics in New York didn't really like *Oliver!* The Artful Dodger was played by seventeen-year-old Davy Jones, who later became a Monkee, and the role of Nancy was played by Georgia Brown, who at the time was a big star. We go out on the road with Davy Jones, and an actress from England named Judy Bruce replaces Georgia Brown. [Dad starts to sing the song "As long as he needs me..."] After a couple of weeks of touring, we're playing a six- week engagement in Chicago. It's dangerous because Claudia Cassidy is the critic for the *Chicago Tribune* and she didn't like the show in New York, so we're nervous. Merrick's new production manager is now Biff Liff—the famous Biff Liff—and Biff and I are friends. This is his first big year working for Merrick and we're in Chicago setting up the show.

On the day of the opening at two o'clock in the afternoon, the phone rings and it's Judy Bruce and she's in the hospital. She turned on the stove in her apartment and it blew up. It burned her hair, eyebrows, eyelashes, and that's the horrible information we get. The understudies at the time were not really very good because Merrick didn't pay anybody a lot of money. Merrick is coming to see the show tonight and Judy Bruce's understudy is going on and the show will be reviewed. We think this is going to be one of the worst nights of our lives.

The phone rings at three o'clock from the hospital and it's Judy Bruce. She says, "I'll make it. Get me a hairpiece and let me do the sound check first."

In those days they put microphones in the footlights. So she arrives at five o'clock and she's got burns on her face, but somebody comes in and gives her a hairpiece, eyelashes and makeup that covers the burns. This was just an okay company who gave a hell of a performance that night that was never repeated again. The cast's energy was on fire because this woman was able to go on the stage with a burnt face and give a crackerjack performance, having just come from the hospital. You knew it from the minute she made her entrance that she was going to be spectacular.

Merrick is sitting in the sixth-row center, and he is a little deaf by the way, and Biff and I know that. Biff and I would take turns sitting at the top of the aisle because we knew that he was going to complain that he couldn't hear the show. So he'd come up the aisle and say, "Make it louder." I would pretend to go and make it louder, which I didn't do, and then we would change positions and Biff would stand at the top of the aisle and pretend to run backstage.

The show is over, and the audience goes nuts because some people there know that Judy Bruce is delivering this performance having just come from the hospital. The critic, Claudia Cassidy, and you can look this up, said she didn't like it in New York, but she loved it in Chicago, except that it was too loud.

When I was on the road with *Oliver!* you traveled by train. Everybody got a little cabinette. I forget what they called it—it's like a closet, but it's private. So when you traveled across the country from New York to San Francisco, that's a three-night trip, it's an exciting train ride. There's a poker game that never stops and people are having affairs with people they never would have... Ya know, you didn't knock on anyone's door because you didn't know who might be inside...

The scenery and costumes are put on baggage cars. If you're the company manager, every time the train stops, even in the middle of the night, you get off and you make sure the baggage car is still on the train. You make sure they don't take your baggage car off by mistake when they take the cattle car off, so it made every company manager very nervous. Evidently there was that great moment when they switched baggage cars, and the costumes from *Gypsy* wound up in Atlanta, and the circus wound up in San Francisco. The company manager from *Gypsy* turned around and the baggage car had giraffes in it.

When I returned from the *Oliver!* tour, I was still the youngest manager at the Merrick office. I did not have any ambition to produce. When I first went out on the road, I got 325 dollars a week with per diem and the second time I got 350 dollars a week. The old-line managers were getting a little more, I guess. I actually did a good job. I knew that I was responsible for the show on the stage and off the stage.

When I came back into the office after being on the road with *Oliver!* they offered me the touring company of *Hello, Dolly!* which was a giant hit.

I remember saying, "Now?! I just came back! I can't go back out again!"

And Jack Schlissel said, "We'll pay you anything you want—450 dollars."

I couldn't take it. The irony was your mother auditioned for the show in Seattle. That show went to Vietnam to entertain the troops and it had Mary Martin in it. In any case, I didn't do it.

It was like a whirlwind of three or four years of theatrical activity which took me away from home, but I became a road expert. You're in the room where it's happenin'. The company manager was not a clerk in those days. He was kind of a part of the game. I would get paid and get a free room, sometimes in garbage hotels, but you could live on the per diem. You could send a check home and you made a living.

I did a show with Merrick called *Sunday in New York*, at the Golden Theatre on West 45th Street, and it ran the season. It's a comedy by some California writers and playing the featured role is a guy named Robert Redford and we become friends. He was making 300 dollars a week and I was making 225 dollars a week and we hung out. We drank coffee together, we played softball together, and we were going to change the world, as young people would do in their conversations, and that was the beginning of my friendship with Redford that has lasted till now. He was young and he had just come in from California. You knew that this man was going to be a star. He was young, handsome, all-American, but also a good guy.

Years later, when he came back to New York to do *Barefoot in the Park,* he had an apartment on East 86th Street, and since he was a Western guy, he decided that his apartment should have a Western look. There was a wall in between the dining room and living room and he wanted to knock out the wall and put in an iron wall instead. I was in disbelief, and I thought I was listening to a lunatic. I asked, "Why?!"

He said, "It's what I want."

I asked, "Where are you going to get all of this material?"

He said, "I know where. On the ground floor, on the windows of Park Avenue, there are these iron gates. Let's go get them."

We were young and a little crazy, so he rented a station wagon and at two o'clock in the morning we unscrewed the metal, loaded it up on top of the station wagon, and he ultimately replaced the wall with iron gating between the two rooms. So that's twice now I'm a felon—the first time with Roy Somlyo and now with Redford. It was bohemian and it was crazy. And that was the beginning of Redford. It becomes important because it was Redford that ultimately introduced me to Neil Simon.

Anyway, there was a group of people who became friends at the Merrick office—Redford, Gene Wolsk (a fellow manager), and me. Gene helped Frank Gilroy out when he wrote the Pulitzer Prize-winning play, *The Subject Was Roses*, and Frank became a part of the group. Gene was friendly with Jim Goldman who had written the play *The Lion in Winter*. Jim Goldman's brother, Bill, wrote *Butch Cassidy and the Sundance Kid.* All these young guys become a part of the group. This group became the social center for some of these artists.

As Gene and I worked on more and more shows, more people would join the group—people like Dustin Hoffman, Hal Holbrook,

Ulu Grosbard, Alan Arkin—and now all of a sudden, it's an elite group. The rest of us were kind of schleppers. It was kind of a loose pseudo chic, ya know... we were very proud of who we were... kind of thing. On Thanksgiving we would go up to Ruth and Frank Gilroy's, play basketball, and celebrate the holiday. Ruth was a great hostess and Frank was one of us. He was from the Bronx.

So I had a job at the Merrick office, and I was now able to stay in the city for a while. I was the company manager of various shows in New York, and I also prepared a lot of shows to go on the road which I think I did pretty well. Merrick did a lot of shows with Tony Richardson, a very successful director, and as time went on, I worked on a lot of those shows. That led to doing a play called *The Milk Train Doesn't Stop Here Anymore*, written by Tennessee Williams, and starring Tallulah Bankhead, Ruth Ford, and Tab Hunter.

Doing a show with Tony Richardson, Tennessee Williams, and Tallulah Bankhead turned out to be a memorable experience for me. Just for the record, Tennessee Williams was drunk most of the time. At eleven o'clock in the morning he was unconscious, never mean, just silly, and he also had a little dog.

Tallulah Bankhead was not the beautiful Tallulah Bankhead anymore—she was one of the wicked witches. When she wanted something, she summoned you to her dressing room, and she would be naked. This was not an easy sight to look at because she smoked and had cigarette burns on her body. She'd keep you in her dressing room until she got what she wanted.

She summoned the production manager, Neil Hartley, an elegant North Carolinian. Neil knew what was going to happen. He would go into the dressing room and try to stare straight ahead, knowing full well that if his eyes dropped, he had to give in to her. Tallulah got what she wanted 95% of the time because none of us could keep from looking down and then we rushed out of the dressing room.

In addition, there were some other shows that I worked on. *The Man in the Glass Booth*, with Donald Pleasence, written by Robert... (he was in *Jaws*... plays the boat captain... Robert Shaw!) and directed by Harold Pinter. Another show I did was with Ben

Gazzara. It was a play called *Traveler Without Luggage* by Jean Anouilh. I also did *Foxy* with Bert Lahr. It opened just about the same time as *Hello, Dolly!* so nobody remembers that show, but it was choreographed by Jack Cole. Did I ever tell you the Jack Cole story?

In my career, I wound up doing a lot of dance shows with a great delusion that I actually knew something about dance, which I didn't. When you grow up in the Bronx, you know nothing about dance. The idea of ballet was as foreign as Norway. We were in Detroit at the Fisher Theatre on the way to New York with *Foxy,* and Jack Cole was the choreographer. Now, I didn't know who Jack Cole was. I was just the company manager and Jack Cole was somewhat of a legend among dancers. He sort of began jazz dancing and he was a mentor to Bob Fosse, but I didn't know anything about that.

Every night I would do the count-up of the tickets that were sold, and I would exit the box office at about the same time that Jack Cole would angrily exit the theatre into the lobby. He felt that he never had enough time to rehearse his numbers, and he always left the theatre when this number was happening during a performance. This happened two or three times and we would bump into each other, and we would say hello. Ya know, he's the choreographer and I'm just the company manager.

One day he looked at me and he said out of nowhere, "I'll have you a leaping contest."

He had nothing to do, and he was beside himself. There are ramps leading up toward the mezzanine and you can leap and jump to touch the ramps and try to touch the mezzanine until you can't touch it anymore. You start at about nine feet and end at about ten and a half feet. So, I was twenty-nine years old, and Jack Cole was this great choreographer, and I said, "Mr. Cole, I'm somewhat of an athlete, I can go up in the air."

He said, "Come on."

Well, I beat him by about a foot, which was nothing but a challenge to him. Next, he lined up all the trash cans in the Fisher Theatre lobby and we had to hurdle them. This challenge ended up being a tie but then there was the intermission, so we had to just stand around and wait for the audience to go back into the theatre.

Then he said, "Okay, I'm standing at one end of the lobby and you're at the other end and we run into each other and the first one to go down, wins."

I thought the man was crazy, but I said, "Okay, you win."

For some reason, we became somewhat friendly, and at the time I still had no idea that the dancers adored him even though he was a tyrant. He had a huge reputation for being mean and tough, but dancers wanted to work for him. Dancers and choreographers are strange people.

So back in New York, he would come over to the house for dinner. We went to the Moiseyev Dance Company. I thought he would go crazy watching these real macho Russian dancers pound the deck. One night we went to P.J. Clarke's for dinner. It was crowded and there was a line at the bar, and he reached over for a beer and some guy called him a "faggot."

Jack Cole probably weighed 120 pounds, and Jack hit the guy and the guy went straight down, but Jack didn't stop there. He jumped on top of him and was beating him up. I had to pull him off.

Later on, he choreographed a show called *Man of La Mancha* and he called me up one day and he asked, "Would you come down and see it?"

It was trying out downtown on West 4th Street in a tent before it moved uptown. I remember going down and seeing it and I thought it was good and I thought his choreography was good.

After the show he was standing there and he asked, "What do you think?"

I said, "It's gonna be a smash."

He looked at me and said, "It's shit."

I said, "Okay, Jack, it's shit, but it's gonna be a smash."

When I was working for Merrick, I always thought that I got the tough shows, and *Foxy* was one of them. Billy Rose, who was a famous producer and married to Fanny Brice, said in a newspaper column that if he were the producer of *Foxy*, it would be a hit. Merrick didn't like Billy Rose and he said that he would sell *Foxy* to him for 10,000 dollars because Billy Rose had a big mouth.

Billy Rose called up and wanted to know what the show cost, the break even, etc... and they asked me to prepare the budget. So when

I went into the theatre that night, Billy Rose asked me to come up to his mansion on top of his theatre—he's got a private elevator.

I sit down and he starts asking me questions and I see underneath his elbow are my budgets that I prepared. He's pumping me to see if what the Merrick office sent over was accurate. Did they lie to him? I really didn't like him because I knew how he treated his staff. So we finished the session and in the elevator on the way down I said, "Mr. Rose, I prepared those numbers." I had a lot of chutzpah in those days.

I also prepared *Artuo Ui* to go to London, but it never went. I thought that it was a brilliant production. It was gonna go to the Royal Court, and I had never been to London before, and I prepared everything. I knew where every piece of scenery and where every costume was going. Then, on Thursday November 22nd, 1963, Merrick's number-one investor, a guy named Max Brown, walked into the office and said, "The President's been shot."

I remember saying, "President of what?"

He said, "Kennedy was shot."

By three o'clock that afternoon, doing a play was not that important, and *Artuo Ui* never went to London. The self-importance that we all had about what the theatre was, or the artistic importance of the theatre, seemed to fade in light of such a political tragedy.

In 1964, my second daughter, Lisa, was born and we moved to a larger apartment. It was a very busy life. I got to the Merrick office at ten o'clock in the morning, I went for dinner, I covered the show and then I went home. That was a ten-hour day, but I knew what I was doing.

There was a community in New York. There were certain restaurants that you ate in, and there was an exchange of information in those restaurants with the other managers because everybody talked to each other. The chorus kids went to Joe Allen's and the managers went to Fornos, Downey's, Sardi's, and Capri, the Italian place. It was a healthy time. By then I was thirty or thirty-one and I was making a living. Sometimes I would get two weeks of work as a house manager at the New York State Theater, which is now the Koch Theater. I did bits and pieces of things that kept expanding my understanding of the business.

I must have done sixteen or seventeen shows with Merrick in one form or another, so I learned a lot. I thought that Merrick was genuinely insane. He was a narcissistic, egomaniacal man living in a fantasy world, but he had taste. Some of the things he did were perverse and lunatic, and just public relations stunts, but he was smart.

I think Merrick bet on the jockey and not on the horse. He was smart enough to hire the talent, but he would not be a famous producer without the talent he hired. So if Tennessee Williams wrote a play, Merrick did it. If Tony Richardson wanted to direct a play, he did it. If Gower Champion wanted to do a musical, he did it. It's also a major lesson—that the people who do the creative work in the theatre, *they* are the stars. The producer can run the press agent and get his name in the paper all day long, but a real producer coordinates between all the elements. The creative personnel and the interpretive creators (the directors, actors, dancers) are the lifeblood. Even then I knew this to be true, because Gower Champion was really good. He was a terror, but he was good. Tony Richardson knew what he was doing. They didn't fake it and they had ideas.

The perverse part was that Merrick didn't want anybody else to have success. He said, "Not only do I have to have all the successes, but everybody else has to fail."

7 WOLSK AND AZENBERG

At some point Gene Wolsk said that it was time for us to open our own office. There was an article in *The New York Times* that said, "Merrick protégées starting their own..." Gene said he wanted to produce, and I would be his general manager, so we left the Merrick office. Gene and I ended up managing a show called *The Impossible Years* starring Alan King and produced by David Black and Walter Hyman. It was a terrible comedy, but people wanted to see Alan King. We became friendly with Alan King and Walter Hyman, who became producing partners with us later. The show ran over a year, so there was a salary.

In that period, we were also going to put on *The Lion in Winter*, written by Jimmy Goldman. What then happened was.... Gene struggled with raising the money and I said that I would help him. I didn't really know how to help him. I think the capitalization was 150,000 dollars, which couldn't get you a sandwich today. So without thinking, I said, "Well, I'll help." I don't know.... whatever.

I went over to my friends and said, "Give me 200 dollars." So I probably helped raise 50,000 dollars, so my name goes up there. I did not know anything about producing, other than having been in the room and seen lunatics like Alex Cohen and David Merrick. It was naive but there it was. Gene and I had an office in the Sardi building which was as big as your old room [very small].

Hal Holbrook was a friend of ours and he had a show called *Mark*

Twain Tonight! He performed it off Broadway and in other small venues.

While we're preparing for *The Lion in Winter*, Hal came into the office one day and asked, "What are you doing?"

I said, "We're doing Jimmy Goldman's show."

Holbrook said, "Why don't you do me?!" which was a funny line at the time. It has a different expression and meaning now.

I remember turning to Gene and I asked, "You wanna do him?"

And Gene asked, "How much does doing him cost?"

We joked about that, and we figured out that in order to produce Hal Holbrook in *Mark Twain Tonight!* on Broadway, it would cost 35,000 dollars. Well, we didn't have 35,000 dollars but we said, "Okay, let's do him!" It was funny.

We borrowed 5,000 dollars from Byron Goldman, a Merrick investor, to put up the Actor's Equity bond for Hal Holbrook whose salary was 125 dollars a week. Everything else we owed... don't ask. We announced Hal Holbrook in *Mark Twain Tonight!* at the Longacre Theatre. There was no big advance sale and I think tickets were $7.50 for the best seats in the house.

In the 1960s, Walter Kerr was a major critic. The opening line of his review said, "I went to see Hal Holbrook in *Mark Twain Tonight!* and after twenty minutes, I wondered when his next book would be coming out." It was a rave notice and people lined up to see it. Whoever heard of such a thing? I don't know what we would have done if it had failed. What Holbrook did with Mark Twain was legendary. He did seven performances a week because it took him three hours to put the makeup on to become Mark Twain.

He would do one matinée a week. We made him extend for three weeks and he was exhausted. I think we beat him up because we were selling out—we turned away a thousand people on the closing night. I wound up doing *Mark Twain Tonight!* three or four times. I did it during the Vietnam War, and then I did it again five or six years ago. When we did it the first time it cost 35,000 dollars. When I did it the third time it cost a million dollars—shows you some strange economics. My share of the profit was equal to Gene's, and we made 7,500 dollars each, which was more money than we'd ever seen.

Hal Holbrook won the Tony for best actor and Rosemary Harris won the Tony for best actress in *The Lion in Winter* and that was our first year. *The Lion in Winter* only ran eleven weeks, but over the twenty years in stock and amateur performances it paid back the investment, which was only 150,000 dollars. The *New York Times* critic that reviewed *The Lion in Winter* was Stanley Kauffmann. He was only at the *Times* for a year or two and then he went on to Yale to screw that place up too. He hated that play, and when the movie came out, he found it "equally odious and loathsome." The movie won the Academy Award... so much for that critic.

It was only Walter Kerr who wrote an encouraging notice to Jimmy Goldman. He told Jimmy that he should write more plays and that he was good, but Walter Kerr was only writing for *The Herald Tribune*. The article was very encouraging to Jimmy, and I remember he cried. You can't fault a critic for having an opinion, but you can fault a newspaper for picking some very limited critics. *The New York Times*, subsequent to Brooks Atkinson, picked Taubman and Kauffmann and they were not qualified, or they were limited or too opinionated.

That was virtually the last play that Jimmy Goldman wrote. He said, "That was the best I had," and that he's not going to do this anymore. He did write *Follies*, and he wrote another play that George Scott might have done called *They Might Be Giants*, but he became a screenwriter like his brother. It was one of the indications of what was happening to the theatre. These young writers, like Bill and Jimmy Goldman or Paddy Chayefsky, are gonna go write for the screen because the theatre was too tough. This was all 1966 or 1967... Right...

At about that time, another show called *The Investigation* came along. Ulu Grosbard sent a script over, which was a transcript of the Frankfurt Auschwitz trial, written by Peter Weiss. Ulu said, "Let's do this play."

It was a three-and-a-half-hour play, which we eventually cut down to two and a half hours. You know you have to say yes to this play because you'd be a coward if you didn't say yes in those days. The four of us, Alan King, Walter Hyman, Gene Wolsk, and I, agree to do the play, but how are we going to get the money? I said let's get 125 people to put up 1,000 dollars each. I'm not sure that we did, but we got a lot of people to put up 1,000 dollars, including Bobby Kennedy.

The director, Ulu Grosbard, is a guy who got out of Belgium as a child right before the Nazis came. He was Elia Kazan's assistant on some films, directed *The Subject Was Roses,* which won the Pulitzer Prize and the Tony Award, and he's a nice guy. We do *The Investigation,* and the preparation took us four or five months and we were constantly involved in the details of the horror of that concentration camp. We met people who were witnesses, it was... The plus part was that we felt that there was an obligation to do good theatre.

The first night of the performance we invite all the Rabbis in New York. The word "Jew" is not mentioned in the play. Peter Weiss, the playwright, was a communist from Germany or Poland or somewhere and he was a Jew, but the point of *The Investigation* is that it's about inhumanity which is worldwide. Well, the arguments afterwards from the Rabbis about why the play didn't mention the word "Jew" went all the way up to Elie Wiesel, who is a Holocaust survivor, and a big-time writer. Ulu and Elie Wiesel argued in the lobby of the Ambassador Theatre.

There was one little man that I remember who stood quietly on the side while all of the arguments were going on. He came over to us at the end of the arguments and he said, "I was there. And this is good."

The show ran eleven weeks on Broadway, and for whatever reason, NBC wanted to do it on television. The money that NBC paid put the show into profit. So that's the third play that we produce, and it turns out to be profitable. I don't mean that Gene and I made a lot of money, but it's putting us on the map. The show makes a 17% profit and now we've moved up a peg, but we're still the young schleppers. We now have an artistic success in *The Lion in Winter* but it's a financial failure. We have a success with Hal Holbrook, and we have two Tony winners so that's pretty good.

While we're doing all of this, we're also general managing some other shows like *George M!,* starring Joel Grey and Bernadette

Peters, and that's how we made a living.

In the summer of 1968, or whatever it was, Jimmy Nederlander Sr., who owned the Palace Theatre, called me up because he wanted to hire me to be the company manager of *Judy Garland at the Palace.*

Well, Judy Garland was on the way down and she had a reputation. It wasn't a terrible one, it was just that she stayed in the theatre until about three o'clock in the morning. There were pills, booze, and everybody catered to her, and you could never get her out of the theatre.

Jimmy Nederlander Sr. said, "I don't care if you go backstage at all, but just make sure that Sid Luft doesn't peddle tickets to the brokers."

So I said okay because it was a good salary and I had two children.

I rarely went backstage, and I kept an eye on the box office and Sid Luft. The show turned out to be a huge success. She was in her own world and the adulation that she got from the predominantly gay audience, who were in love with her... they didn't care if she hit the notes or not. Up until now, I had no concept of what Judy Garland meant in the gay world. It was an experience beautifully described in Bill Goldman's book *The Season.* It was a theatrical event and even though she was on the way down it was a huge success. I was glad I was there. When you think that I did shows with Lena Horne, Barbara Cook, Barbra Streisand, and Judy Garland—it's not terrible. Talking about it now, it sounds like romantic Broadway history, but it was a normal day.

Then Carl Reiner sent a script over called *Something Different.* It starred Bob Dishy and Linda Lavin, and Carl directed it. Carl Reiner was famous, and he was the nicest guy. *Something Different* was about a play within a play within a play, but it didn't work. During the third act, the cast that you saw on stage in the first two acts is sitting in the audience watching the play. The show was funny, but it was a mess. I joked about it. I said if we play another two towns, we'll cut the first two acts and we'll have no play—maybe that will be the whole evening.

The famous Groucho Marx came to a matinée and at the end of

the play he stood up and said to the audience, "This is a funny play! Who knows more about what is funny than I do? I think you should give this cast a standing ovation." It was a highlight.

I expected the show to be a success, but it failed. That was naive on my part. Carl dealt with the fact that the play failed like a pro, but I remember feeling very vulnerable and beaten up. I slept late the next day after the opening night and for a week afterward. I didn't want to face the idea of a failed show. I then acknowledged in my head that I would never be that vulnerable again. This is a treacherous business and shows either fail or succeed. I wasn't going to allow myself to feel that way again. You put your heart and soul into your show, and as Terrence McNally says, "It's only a play," and somehow you recover. To a certain extent, I lived up to that, but you are always vulnerable. You're not objective about your own stuff. When I had failures, I paid an interesting price, and I was never jubilant enough with the successes either.

While I worked at the Merrick office, there was a Black stage manager, maybe the only one, named Charlie Blackwell. Charlie Blackwell was 6 foot 5, and 225 pounds with no fat. I'm a white Jewish guy from the Bronx and he's a Black guy from North Carolina and then Philadelphia, and we got along. We would have dinner at cheap Chinese restaurants, and we played softball together. We did a lot of stuff. He was a big-time stage manager, and he did those big musicals of Merrick's, like *Carnival*.

Charlie came in one day with a recording and he played it for Gene and me. It's called *Ain't Supposed to Die a Natural Death* and it's about Black street life—people who are on the streets in Harlem. It's about a kid running away from the cops on a street in a Black ghetto, a hooker, a junkie, a guy who's going to turn into a serial killer, and plain old people. It's all done to jazz riffs written by Melvin Van Peebles.

Charlie said, "We should do this."

So we sat and talked about it and I asked, "How do we do this? There's nothing written."

We had this conversation for a couple of months. There's a Black college in Sacramento and we go out and see it. The college is doing a version of the record and they set the show on monkey bars. We went to see it and it hit us—don't set it on monkey bars, it should be set on the street. These are people walking on the street and you have to stage it so that there's constant activity. Then each person on the street has their moment and they sing their story to a jazz riff.

We're all going to raise the money for this hard-nosed Black play. Gilbert Moses, who was a young Black director, directed it.

The last number is about a woman, a bag lady, who turns to the audience after walking on the stage for the entire evening and says, "Put a curse on you. May all your children be junkies too." It was tough...

Nobody had ever seen a piece like that on Broadway before, and Clive Barnes of *The New York Times* wrote a bad notice. The next day on the radio he apologized and said it was cutting edge and brilliant. Jack Kroll from *Newsweek* wrote that this was a great piece. We got mixed and frightening responses because it was harsh. There was a scene with two cops that wore white masks, but they were played by Black actors. They picked up a prostitute on the street and sang, "Smile, brown sugar," in jazz riffs, "it's Salamaggi's birthday." They were delivering a prostitute to the police precinct captain because it was his birthday.

Nobody ever saw stuff like that before, and it broke even at about 31,000 dollars a week. We never made any money, but it ran a year and it received seven Tony nominations. Young Black women would come by the box office and could only afford 2 or 3 dollars, whatever they had, and we let them see the show. They would bring their kids, but you can't let a five or six-year-old into the theatre to see this play, so Charlie and I babysat their children. We took the kids to the Roxy delicatessen.

Working with Charlie added to my life experience and my theatre experience. I would imagine to a certain extent that Black people and white people working together was not normal. It was normal for us in the theatre, but it wasn't normal for society at that time. My relationship with Charlie Blackwell gave me some credibility in the Black theatre community. If he was friendly with you, then you were okay. We always had an understanding that we could never really walk in each other's shoes, but that we could get closer than most people. Because of that relationship, I was involved with the Black theatre community, and I ended up doing any number of shows, like *The Poison Tree, Master Harold and the Boys, A Hand is on the Gate, Ain't Misbehavin'* and *The Wiz.* We did a lot of shows together and he was my good friend. He died of bad medicine. They misdiagnosed him with bladder cancer, but he said to his wife two days before he died, "It's okay. I've had a great life."

Charlie and I were honest friends and the one thing that was crucial between us was trust, no matter what.

Gene and I became interesting producers. We didn't really make any money and we struggled, but we made ends meet—that's about all. We didn't make any money on *Ain't Supposed to Die a Natural Death* and we didn't make any money on *The Lion in Winter.* We didn't make any money on *Something Different,* but there was a cachet. We were young producers, and we were producing tough stuff because we thought that's what we were supposed to do. Each time and each effort expands your experience.

It's during the first two or three years of our independence from the Merrick office that Gene and I become a part of the Broadway scene. I did seventeen shows for David Merrick as a company manager. Back then, company managers were given much more authority than they are today, and I learned a lot. I learned about the economics of the theatre, and this knowledge gave me confidence as a producer.

Managers may not know so much about the aesthetics and what is going to work and what is not going to work creatively on a show, but we do know about the economics. We understand the relationship between the unions and the management, and the theatre owner and the show. I remember walking down 45th Street when I was thirty-five years old, and I knew that I couldn't be fooled anymore. I conceptually understood the theatre and I couldn't be fooled by all the people with pseudo information about this business. At this point in my career, Gene and I are not Hal Prince and we're not David Merrick. We don't have any big hits but we're in the game. What kind of food do you want for lunch?

8 THE KNICKS, THE STONES, AND BACK TO BROADWAY

Gene and I had been on the cutting edge and now we had become the establishment. After we did a couple of Broadway shows, and I had two children at this point, I got an offer to work at Madison Square Garden. I was offered the job as vice president in charge of production for 35,000 dollars a year, which was more money than I had ever made. This job provided security for my family and season tickets to the Knicks games. This is Madison Square Garden and it's at the time when the Knicks were good. The former general manager of the Shubert Organization, Alvin Cooperman, worked there and he asked me to join him.

I think I was there for seven or eight months, and there were some nice guys. That's where I met Bill Bradley, Red Holzman, and Dave DeBusschere. This is in the very late '60s because the Knicks won the championship that year. The Garden was supposed to become the entertainment center of the world and I'm trying to come up with projects.

A disc jockey came into my office and said he wanted to hold Miss Black America at the Garden. I said, "Okay, we can do that." We sold tickets in the Felt Forum, the smaller venue, and women contestants from Louisiana and Mississippi showed up. Just to be there was important for all those women because it was truly a Black pride event. I also booked any number of rock concerts with James Brown, Wilson Pickett, lots of rock and roll names. What did I know? The Jackson 5 wanted to perform, and they did it for nothing. They were just starting out and I approved it.

Alan Klein, the manager of the Rolling Stones, walked into my office and said that they wanted to play the Garden on Thanksgiving. In those days the Garden took 25,000 dollars plus expenses per night as a fee and you could do whatever you want, so it didn't make any difference to me who was performing, as long as there was a booking. I didn't give a shit about the Rolling Stones. I didn't know one Rolling Stone from another. I already had Sly and the Family Stone booked for Thanksgiving, so I said to Alan Klein, "I got Stones. I got Sly and the Family Stone."

Somehow Alan Klein convinced Sly and the Family Stone not to take the booking, so the Rolling Stones played Thanksgiving at the Garden. I forgot who the opening act was (it was some unknown), and then the next act was B.B. King, followed by Ike and Tina Turner. Janice Joplin, who was in the audience, jumped up on the stage with Ike and Tina Turner and did twenty minutes and she was totally drunk. The place was going nuts.

In those days people smoked marijuana indoors. People on the bottom floor of the Garden would smoke and the people up at the top wouldn't have to smoke because the smoke floated up to the top and they were unconscious. Then I heard my name paged over the sound system. The stagehands that were working there, like my friend Paul DeSavino, thought that was great. Manny is being paged. It's like being paged playing for the Knicks.

"And now going in to play for the Knicks...."

Ya know what I mean? I think it's a joke. So I go down to the floor and there's Alan Klein who says, "I want 25,000 dollars more and 5% of the gross or the Stones don't go on."

When the stagehands heard my name being paged, they were there, they wanted to see what was going on. I remember I was so furious. I said to Alan Klein, "You mean to say that if I don't give you 25,000 dollars, you will cancel the concert?"

He said, "Yeah."

I said, "No. I will cancel the concert."

I said to Paul DeSavino, "Don't let anybody on the stage without my okay."

Alan saw all these big strong guys pick up pieces of metal and take their watches off and he said, "What'd you do? Bring your own mafia?"

I said, "I don't need them for you. You'd be mine. And I don't know where I'd get 25,000 dollars at midnight on Thanksgiving, but even if I could, you wouldn't leave the building with it."

So the Stones did go on, and on Monday Paul DeSavino came into the office and said, "You know they filmed it and they made a recording of it. What do I charge them?"

They recorded three concerts, so normally there would be three recording fees. I said, "Make it twelve recording fees."

So on Thursday when Alan Klein got the big bill, he called me up and said, "Uh, you have to help me out. I got a big stagehand bill."

I said, "You put a gun to my head last Thursday and those guys would have saved my life. I'll see you in court."

He ultimately went to jail for other less-than-legal business practices in other venues. But that was a hell of a concert. It became *Gimme Shelter*, the movie.

When we saw how good the Knicks were, Bill Goldman, who wrote *Butch Cassidy and the Sundance Kid*, wanted to do a documentary film. It would be a film following the Knicks during the seasons where they might become the champions. It would be narrated by Robert Redford and Dustin Hoffman. They both said that they would do it without getting paid, as long as they had the right to buy two seats for the Knicks games. In that year, the single and biggest form of entertainment in New York was the Knicks games. Very well-dressed crowds went, and it was euphoria. Everyone looked forward to the games—the Knicks were a great team.

When this idea was presented, it was going to cost nothing. The only cost would be for Bill Goldman to travel with the team on two road trips. At this point in time, Bill Goldman had won the Academy Award, Robert Redford was the "Sundance Kid," and Dustin Hoffman had done *The Graduate*. We had giants, and all they wanted in return was to watch the ball game. For whatever reason, the Garden turned it down. I said to my friend, Bob Malina, who also worked with me at the Garden, "If they say no to this, then what could they possibly say yes to? This is brainless and it costs nothing."

When the Garden said no to the Redford project, I knew that the idea of Madison Square Garden becoming the entertainment center of the world and expanding into theatre and film was probably not going to happen. I left the Garden and returned to the theatre. My relationship with the Garden was fine. So much so, that a few years later I was offered the presidency. I said, "Yes, but on certain conditions." I couldn't work for certain people because they didn't know anything about the logistics—stagehands, labor, etc... They were all nice enough people, but I decided that I didn't want to work there. They offered me 90,000 dollars, which was like a fortune of money, but I returned to the theatre.

Hilly Elkins, a Broadway agent and producer, whom I knew from Kinderwelt, was going to produce a show called *The Rothschilds.* This would be the Bock and Harnick musical after *Fiddler on the Roof.*

Bob Malina said to me, "See if Hilly Elkins has got jobs for the two of us."

Hilly asked, "How much money do you want?"

I said, "I want 125,000 dollars a year, split between Bob Malina and me."

Hilly said okay, and I left the Garden to become the general manager of *The Rothschilds*.

Needless to say, we never got paid. Hilly didn't have the money. He just said, "Sure."

I think I made 18,000 dollars that year. The show was going to be produced by Lester Osterman, who was a Broadway guy, and Hilly Elkins. They may have argued about their own billing more than anything else. The original director was Derek Goldby, and the original choreographer was Eliot Feld. Eliot Feld left the show because he wanted to direct, and that's when Michael Kidd got the job. Michael Kidd and I became very good friends. It was a conspiracy between Michael and me to overcome the egos of everyone and to put some sort of practicality into what we were doing. There was no chief. The problem with the play was that Mayer Rothschild, played by Hal Linden, died at the end of the first act and everybody had fallen in love with him.

As the general manager, you have to suppress any artistic suggestions that you have, and also, I had no interest in getting in between these crazy people. So we do a run-through at the Lunt-Fontanne Theatre and there is a meeting afterwards where everyone is yelling at each other.

Somebody said, "We don't have a ballet, we need a ballet!"

I stopped everybody from leaving the meeting and I said, "Wait a minute. You want to put together a ballet for Detroit in a week?! We're going to need new scenery, new costumes, we only have 80,000 dollars left, and it will wipe us out."

For whatever reason, they agreed because I think everybody knew that was the right answer, except it was coming from the general manager.

The next day, Jerry Bock came down the aisle in the theatre and asked, "Was that an artistic decision? Or a financial decision?" As if I would intrude on the artistic decisions.

I remember I was sensible enough to say, "A financial decision, Jerry!"

And he went, "Oh."

We went to Detroit and the "Gold Smugglers Ballet" was never heard from again. Derek Goldby was ultimately fired, and Michael Kidd took over as director/choreographer.

The show ran a year, and your mother was in the chorus. For me, it was my second big experience with a major league choreographer. First, there was Jack Cole and now Michael Kidd. They were big-time and I began to know a little more about dance. Michael had a brain. He wasn't just a hoofer and I really liked him. We got along for the next thirty years, and it was one of those relationships that sustained and didn't end with the show. I gave the eulogy at his funeral. Michael and I got along forever—we were genuine friends.

I made a living from general management because I was knowledgeable. Producing I did, but the bills were paid from the general management—there was no shame in it. One day the phone rang. It was Ken Harper, a disc jockey, who had an idea to do *The*

Wizard of Oz with an all-Black cast, and he began to develop the music for the show with a composer named Charlie Smalls. They presented the score to Twentieth Century Fox who wanted to produce it because they would also control the music. They loved the score, but Ken Harper had never produced anything before, so they asked me if I would produce the show but not take producer billing. They are going to put up all the money and I will be billed as the general manager.

I said, "Sure."

I'll get a percentage of the profit, a percentage of the gross, and all of that. Gilbert Moses who directed *Ain't Supposed to Die a Natural Death* is going to direct it and Geoffrey Holder is going to do the costumes. It starred Stephanie Mills, Ken Page and André de Shields.

We go to Detroit to try out, and there's something wrong with the show. Stephanie Mills can really sing and blows everybody away when she sings "Home," the big song, but the show is not a success—something is not happening. Gilbert Moses gets fired and Geoffrey Holder takes over. The show then moves to Philadelphia and the guy playing the Scarecrow gets sick so the understudy, Hinton Battle, goes on. The Scarecrow was played by a Black comedian who had a dance number, but he couldn't dance, so with Hinton Battle in the part, all of a sudden you knew that's what the Scarecrow was supposed to be. From that moment on, the show was something else. It was amazing.

Now this is a show for both a Black and white audience, but it's going to take time to build. We go into New York, open the show, and the notices are only okay. From a white point of view, it wasn't *A Chorus Line,* but it had authenticity for a Black audience and every day the ticket sales kept growing a little. I went to the advertising agency, and I gave specific instructions. I said that we were not going to spend hundreds of thousands of dollars for ads in *The New York Times*. This show was going to arrive the way shows arrive, by word of mouth.

Twentieth Century Fox was nervous, so they sent one of their guys down, who I didn't like, to the ad agency. Two or three days later, I visited the ad agency and I saw on the table, a full-page ad for *The Wiz* in *The New York Times*. I asked, "Who did that?!"

Now, I'm the chief. Ken Harper, who supported me, was there and I remember diving over the table at the Twentieth Century Fox guy with my fist swinging, saying, "Get this shit out of here! This show is going to make it, but it's going to make it on its own!"

It was successful because of its own word of mouth. It toured and it became one of those shows with its own kind of history. It was good and it showed Black talent.

As a producer, sometimes 90% of your function is managerial. If you're doing a show with Tom Stoppard or with Mike Nichols, you better be on top of the management because that is your only strength and that impacts the artistic stuff. If your show's weekly operating costs break even at 20,000 dollars a week less, that saving will provide jobs for an extra three months for fifty people, and you might actually make money. If you're spending 10,000 dollars a week more in your weekly operating costs, that's a half a million dollars at the end of the year. I wasn't in what used to be called the "weekly business." I made money when everybody else made money.

9 "HOW'D YOU LIKE TO PRODUCE MY PLAYS?"

It was about that time that Neil Simon called up. I met Neil in 1962, on the *Barefoot in the Par*k Broadway Softball League team. Neil's recollection was that he played centerfield, but he didn't. He played second base. Neil wanted to play centerfield like Joe DiMaggio, but he didn't. Redford played first base, I played shortstop, and that's how I met Neil. My career with Neil had nothing to do with the theatre. It actually had to do with being on a softball team. I thought I was a good player. I thought it was the one thing I could actually do—I was a good schoolyard ball player.

Neil at the time was a big star. He wrote *Barefoot in the Park*, starring Redford, and *The Odd Couple*. Those were giant hits, and *The Odd Couple* became... you know... iconic. Then he did *Plaza Suite,* so he had three hits in a row that got rave notices. Ellie and I were invited to the opening nights, and Neil and I were friendly enough. In those days the opening night was one big night. You put on a tuxedo, all the critics came that night, and if you said you were going to the opening night of a Broadway show, that was an enviable thing. [Dad snaps his fingers, showing me how chic those nights were.] It wasn't like now, where two thousand people attend the party. This was two or three hundred people, or it was a small private dinner.

Between 1963 and 1970 we would have dinner with Neil and Joan Simon on occasion. It's hard to remember what that was like because he was Neil Simon, he was the king of Broadway, and we were regular people. I still had connections at the Garden, and Neil and I went to the Knicks games which was also an enviable social event. I did not have any fantasies about being his producer. Maybe I had a 2% envy of what it would be like, but it never came up. It was never discussed. Neil wrote hit comedies, three giant ones, and I think they were all on Broadway at the same time.

Then he did a bad play, called *The Star-Spangled Girl,* and Walter Kerr's review was, "Neil Simon didn't have a play to write for us this year, but he wrote one anyway." It wasn't very good, but it was forgiven because the other plays were genuine hits. Writing comedy is not simple, it's hard. I was friendly with Neil, but at this point it's a friendship without having any thoughts of a partnership or collaboration. He was a celebrity, but he was also a guy from the Bronx with "the old neighborhood" sensibilities.

Then Neil wrote *The Gingerbread Lady,* which was his effort to write a serious play. When it opened in New Haven, it got good notices. It was about a woman who drinks, and the film is called *Only When I Laugh.* The lead in *The Gingerbread Lady* was Maureen Stapleton, who was a first-rate actress. Everyone thinks, "Hey! It's good!" and then they take the show to Boston and the play gets bad notices. They got frightened and they're gonna close it and not bring it to New York.

When they announced that they were closing the show, they lost all of their theatre parties. The story that goes around is that Maureen Stapleton said to Neil, "You close the show and I'll kill you."

Neil did a big rewrite and he made it funnier, which was indicative of what Neil did when he got nervous. He made it funnier instead of making it more genuine. The show came to New York, and Ellie and I were invited to the opening night.

Joan Simon came over to me at the party and she asked, "How'd you like to produce his plays?"

I hugged her and I said, "Don't worry, the notices are going to be better than you think," which I really believed, and they were.

She broke away from the hug and said, "Somebody has to tell him the truth," which was apparently not happening. If you were connected to Neil in any way, you made a lot of money because he had hits, so nobody told him the truth. I think that was the show where Joan punched the press agent. That was the end of that moment.

A few years later, Neil is back on track with *The Prisoner of Second Avenue*, which was a success. When you think of what kind of career Neil Simon had—I could be wrong by one, but I think he had twenty-two successes and seventeen were hits. It was unheard of. Neil traveled in a circle with people like Mike Nichols, Comden and Green, Bob Fosse, and Gwen Verdon. Nichols was Neil's director for the most part. I'm producing artsy craftsy shows, but I had worked for the Merrick office. I had a good reputation on a level that Neil never knew about. This was about the crew, the stagehands, the practicality, the managerial stuff. Or maybe he did know... I don't know.

I guess I was a decent sounding board and then, in 1969 or 1970, on Memorial Day, the phone rang in my apartment on Central Park West.

Neil asked, "Would you come over?"

When I arrived, he was standing there with a script. He said, "How'd you like to produce my plays?"

[Dad then speaks to me and says...] You're a performer, so you know...

"How would you like to star in my next musical on Broadway?" It was... How can you...? You're talking about the biggest name on Broadway, and he turns to you and really all I've done is three or four shows.

I was funny but I was not as funny as he was, and I remember saying, "I don't know, let me think about it," because I thought this was kind of a funny scene.

He wasn't laughing. He literally threw a script at me, and he said, "Read it and let me know what you think."

That was it. I said, "I'll go home and read it and I'll call you right away."

I walked home from East 62nd Street to West 92nd Street through Central Park. I don't think I touched the ground. That play was *The Sunshine Boys*.

The Sunshine Boys is about old-line Vaudevillians, and their time is up. It's twenty years later and they are retired but there's an effort to bring them back on *The Ed Sullivan Show*. The prototypes for them were Gallagher and Shean, who were an old Irish Vaudeville comic duo. In *The Sunshine Boys* they weren't Irish, they were Jewish, and they didn't talk to each other. They performed together but then they didn't talk to each other off-stage. Well, that was Neil's funny idea to write a play about these two guys who didn't talk to each other.

You can watch it with uh... in the film they made... with George Burns and Walter Matthau. The leads in *The Sunshine Boys* on Broadway were Sam Levene and Jack Albertson. Sam Levene was the original Nathan Detroit in *Guys and Dolls*. He was also in *The Impossible Years*, and he hit a kid who was in it. When he slapped the kid, I almost killed him. I threw him up against the wall. I really had my fist to his face. This was a twelve-year-old kid he hit backstage. He was mean.

In those days, a star's contract was 2,500 dollars a week. There was a clause in Equity that's called ... I don't know, I forgot the name of it, whatever it was... the conversion clause! Sam could not say no to this part. I hired him for 1,250 dollars and if we convert him, he gets 2,500 dollars. This meant that for a period of time he was nervous because I wanted him to behave well. Sam Levene was a star, but he was genuinely misanthropic.

Jack Albertson played the other role and he had just come off a television series, so he was a star, but he also had trouble remembering his lines. Sam started to learn his lines six months before rehearsal. He knew everybody's lines. On the opening night in Washington, there's a scene when Jack Albertson's character turns to his nephew who is visiting him and bringing him groceries.

Jack Albertson's character says out of nowhere, "You know what words are funny?" He doesn't wait for an answer, and he says, "Words with a 'K' in it are funny. Cookie is funny, pickle is funny, cucumber is funny. Robert Taylor is not funny. Tomato is not funny. Kai Kai Kyler is a funny name."

It was Neil's thought that words with hard consonants are funnier than words without. Those tiny little bits and pieces are what makes his thinking brilliant. Since there was no lead-in to that line, Jack would forget it, and then you'd be lost in the middle of a scene. It's the opening night in Washington and he forgets the line. The opening night critics are there, including a good critic from *The Washington Post* named Dick Coe. We met with him at one o'clock in the morning and he gently gave us his suggestions. In those days, the critics from Boston and Washington would write their review and you'd have a cup of coffee with them later that night. They wanted to participate, and they weren't antagonistic. There were no dramaturgs. You got the critic.

Well, at the next day's rehearsal, I thought Jack Albertson had a chance of being killed by the playwright and he knew it. Jack comes down to rehearsal where there is dead silence.

Neil had rewritten the scene and he turned to Jack Albertson and said, "Can you remember one fucking line? 'Cause that's all I'm giving you. The line is... 'Do you know what words are funny?' And then the nephew says, 'You told me a million times Uncle Willy, words with a K in it are funny' and then you repeat, 'Words with a K in it are funny'... because you don't listen, so you're going to repeat it."

The nephew cued every line, "Words with a 'K' in it are funny."

Then Jack would say, "Words with a 'K' in it are funny."

"Pickle."

"Pickle is funny."

"Cookie."

"Cookie is funny."

Every part of that scene was cued. It was brilliant. Then, when they got to the last part, they both said, "Robert Taylor is not funny!" as if they had had this conversation six thousand times.

The play was a big success. We converted Sam Levene's contract to 2,500 dollars three weeks early because he had memorized Jack's part and cued him. *The Sunshine Boys* opened, and it ran a couple of years. It toured, and Neil and I got along.

There was a reason Neil asked me to produce his plays. He had just found out that his wife, Joan, was going to die. She had metastasized breast cancer. This was an era in which one would go through radiation, which was a killer. Joan was given a year to live, and she made it through thirteen months. She didn't like Neil's producer, Saint Subber. Over the next year, they were going to clear the decks of anything in her life that they didn't like. He bought a house in Bedford so that they could be close to her treatments and also so that they would be in the country. If you read the book, *Rewrites,* you'll read about that period. It's in that period of time that he wrote his take on some Chekhov stories. Neil and Joan loved Chekhov and he wrote the play, *The Good Doctor*, in effect for her because she was dying. I, of course said, "Yes, I'd love to do it" and Gene Wolsk and I produced it together.

I remember when we went to the opening night of *The Sunshine Boys* in New Haven... we knew that she knew that this was her last opening.

I never quite knew what the dynamics were between Neil and Joan at that time. I think that she didn't want Neil to know that she knew that she was dying because she thought that he couldn't handle it. He simply couldn't deal with the idea that Joan was not going to be there anymore. The idea that here was maybe the most successful playwright in the history of Broadway and his 35-year-old wife, mother of their two children, was going to die... What else mattered? That was that. Six months after *The Sunshine Boys* opened, Joan died. Ellen, the oldest daughter, knew what was going on, but they didn't tell Nancy, the younger daughter, until the last minute. She was ten years old.

Neil wrote *The Good Doctor* while Joan was dying. It had an all-star cast—Christopher Plummer, Marsha Mason, René Auberjonois, Barney Hughes, and Frances Sternhagen. The new hot director of the month, who had just done two successful plays, was A.J. Antoon.

When Marsha Mason came into audition, she gave a hell of an audition, and she got the part. You kind of had a hint of "uh oh..." and Neil and Marsha started dating during rehearsals and Neil wasn't the kind of guy that dates. By the time we were in New Haven, they were necking in the balcony. When we were rehearsing on the stage, they thought they couldn't be seen. Everybody would pretend not to see them. They got engaged quickly.

I delivered the toast and I said, "I hope that the show runs longer than the engagement." Marsha Mason had married Doc Simon but the only woman that married Marvin Neil Simon was Joan, and it was different. Joan was fearless. I think I told you that if everyone went to East Hampton, she went to Spain. If the crowd was going somewhere, she was going somewhere else. I really liked her. She was nutty but she had a head on her shoulders.

Neil and Marsha moved to California and he's writing the film version of *The Sunshine Boys.* He had written a play called *God's Favorite* and it's the one play that I said "no" to, and he dealt with that. It came in and out of the drawer.

After the third or fourth time, I think it must have been a year later, I said "Okay, let's do it."

He asked, "Why?"

And I remember saying, "We'll exorcise it. You're stuck on this play, so let's just do it and get it over with," and we did.

It was the story of Job from the Bible. It was a really angry play because he was angry about his wife dying, and there was nothing he could do about it. He's got all the wealth in the world, and he has the most successful career, but God is going to test his faith. Neil had everything in the world, and it was taken away.

Job was played by Vince Gardenia, who was a first-rate actor.

Charlie Reilly, who was a lovely and funny guy, played the Angel of God who says, "I can't deliver this. This is too much pain. Why do I have to...?"

That was Neil's thing. Why? I have everything and then I lose... Well, doing a comedy about the fifteen pages in the Bible that are the most horrific... Walter Kerr, who liked Neil, said, "This is like a satyr play." The other critics wanted Neil to be funny.

Michael Bennett, who became famous for *A Chorus Line*, directed it. Michael was not a great play director, but the problems were with the play. The show opened and played about four or five months and closed. The play was exorcised.

It was also a sad time. The girls had lost their mother, but it's a tribute to Joan and Marsha that both Ellen and Nancy, who are now in their fifties and sixties, are okay. They are well balanced, and I genuinely feel like an uncle to them.

By now, I'm beginning to learn what the obligations and

complications are of being a producer to a playwright.

Neil would write thirty pages of a play and say to me, "Here. Read this."

I would read it and I would say, "This is good. What happens next?" He would say, "How the hell do I know?"

And it's a lesson. Almost every good playwright is intuitive. It's not well thought out. They write—it's what's called talent. I never told Neil what to write, I just told him if I was engaged. If you tell the playwright what to write, they don't trust you. It's like telling somebody their baby is ugly. You don't do that. You are intruding on something mysterious. These playwrights are serious people making major efforts and there's a certain amount of necessary diplomacy.

Neil would make cuts, but you'd have to wait a week or two before he would take out some of the product jokes or bad lines. And don't bring it up to him because it wastes time.

Neil wrote me a note once that said, "Don't worry, I know how to fix it."

Then we did another play, and he wrote me a note that said, "Worry, I don't know how to fix it."

Neil began to write *California Suite* which is four one-act sketches about four couples staying at the Beverly Hills Hotel—the same way *Plaza Suite* was about the Plaza Hotel. The first sketch, which I thought was good, was with Tammy Grimes and George Grizzard. It's about a guy meeting his ex-wife and they discuss the relationship they had during their marriage.

There's one line that they kept in the film, which I always thought was good. The ex-wife turns to her former husband and asks, "Is falling in love better now than it was?"

And George Grizzard would take a pause and say, "Yes."

With sadness she asks, "Why?"

He says, "Because it's now."

It's a good line. It was kind of a soap opera, ya know... and it was good.

The second sketch was with the actors Jack Weston and Barbara Barrie. He wakes up in bed with a hooker and doesn't remember how she got there. It's one of the funniest sketches ever and it brought the house down. It was an enormous success. Tammy Grimes and George Grizzard were in the third sketch which may be the best one-act that Neil ever wrote.

Maggie Smith and Michael Caine were in the movie, and she won the Academy Award. The first three sketches were about something, and they were terrific. The fourth sketch was no good. It was kind of a farce, but the first three made the evening and the show was a success. That brought Neil back from having two shows that didn't work.

In the long run, I think I was Neil's best friend. I never invested in the fact that he was mine because he was too famous. One of the crucial conditions in our relationship, unlike with the previous producer, was that Neil didn't want me to be dependent on him. He said, "You can produce other things."

It was a big deal because my relationship with Neil Simon allowed me to do all the other stuff. You know, I would be known as Neil Simon's producer, but I did the Stoppard plays, the Fugard play, the Sondheim musical. I did all of those things with Neil's blessing.

10 MY TRUSTED FRIENDS

There was a period of time when I had six shows running on Broadway and I don't even know what I had on the road. When you think about it, it was extraordinary, but it was normal. The essence of how I could do that is that I had sensational production heads. There was Pete Feller and Frank DeVerna, who ran the technical aspects, and David Taylor, Martin Herzer, Peter Lawrence, and Philip Cusack [my godfather] were the stage managers. Jose Vega was the general manager. They had authority and they didn't have too much interpersonal crap. If I wanted to do a play, my joke was that I could throw the script across the room at them, go away, return in a week, and we could go into rehearsal. Everybody went about their business, and nobody thought anything of it.

In the old days, people used to rent their lighting equipment for their shows, usually from one major company called Century Lighting. Along comes my friend, Frank DeVerna, who was also the business agent for Local One, the Broadway stagehands' union. He was a tough guy, a good guy, and he and Pete Feller, a major theatre carpenter, started Four Star Lighting which is gonna compete with Century Lighting. Century would try to drive the price down in negotiations in order to put Four Star Lighting out of business. Gene Wolsk and I were going to stick with Frank DeVerna and Four Star.

When *A Chorus Line* opened downtown at The Public Theater, it was a smash. It moved to the Shubert Theatre, and the lighting equipment was loaded in from Four Star's warehouse.

David Merrick stored his lighting equipment at Four Star's warehouse, and this could have been Merrick's lighting equipment that was being used for *A Chorus Line*, which was not his show. No one knew for sure because accurate records were never kept back in those days.

Merrick sends a sheriff down to the Shubert Theatre with his carpenter, Teddy Van Bemmel. Teddy, who is loyal to David Merrick and afraid of Pete Feller, says that the equipment belongs to Merrick. David Merrick is actually trying to screw up the load-in for Four Star. He was a shit. He was resentful of *A Chorus Line's* success, and he wanted to make trouble. He was a nasty man.

Pete Feller is the carpenter in charge of the load-in. The sheriff walks in with Teddy Van Bemmel, who is 6 foot 4.

Pete Feller asks Teddy, "What are you doing here?"

The sheriff says to Pete, "Take this equipment down. It belongs to David Merrick."

Pete Feller says, "The stagehands put it up and the stagehands will take it down."

Well, all of a sudden there were no stagehands available in New York City to do any work because nobody is going to cross Pete Feller.

The word got around and the Shuberts heard about it. They got an injunction to stop the action and it turned out that the order was forged. David Merrick's lawyer gets banned, but there's a lawsuit against Frank DeVerna. Merrick has a lot of money and Frank has no money to fight the lawsuit.

Frank called me up and said, "Computer boards are just coming out. Buy two computer boards from me."

Each board cost 125,000 dollars and I would send it out on the road since I had a lot of shows at this point. I think I had *Chapter Two* or *They're Playing Our Song* or *Ain't Misbehavin'* on the road, something like that. Tharon Musser (the lighting designer for *A Chorus Line* and most of my shows) and I go down to Joe Papp, the founder of The Public Theater, and we convince Joe that he should buy two boards for the two touring companies of *A Chorus Line*. It pays for itself because the charge is like 2,000 dollars a week, and at the end of the year you have paid for the board, and you own it.

Hal Prince buys one, we buy two, and Joe Papp buys two, which gives Frank 625,000 dollars. It gave him the money to defend the lawsuit, which took seven years to settle but he won. Four Star Lighting was the king of equipment, and everything turned out okay. Frank was a street guy and I stood by him, and because I was loyal to Frank, I never had any trouble. He had a great reputation with management and labor, and he was my friend.

The two great carpentry shops at the time were owned by Pete Feller and Willy Nolan but none of us young guys could get into those shops to get our shows built. You always had to go to a third shop that was never as good as Pete Feller's or Willy Nolan's.

Pete was my friend, so I complained to him. I said, "I can't get my shows into your shop because you are building shows for Hal Prince and David Merrick, so your shop is always occupied."

Pete said, "That's the way it goes. I can't say no to them."

So I said, "I'm going to find my own shop."

A guy named Dick Wright had a rinky dink shop on Long Island, and Gene and I told him that we were going to give him a big show. This will hopefully establish a new shop so that we will have a place to go and not always have to pay triple time in stagehand salaries. That show was *Billy Budd*, which was a big seafaring musical. Ming Cho Lee, the set designer, designed an enormous and very complicated set. The load-in had 36 stagehands working—electrics, carpentry, props, and sound. Those 36 stagehands didn't stop working until the lights were focused, and all the set pieces worked per union rules.

Well, the set pieces weren't working and we're paying these men day after day, and they can't fix them. By the second day, at five o'clock at the stage door, appears the great Pete Feller and two men from his shop. Pete, who is the king, tells everybody in the theatre to get out. He works with his two men until three o'clock in the morning and pushes a button and all the hydraulics finally work.

I stayed there with him, and I said, "I owe you."

He said, "No, you were right. You get me the drawings of the set for your next show before Merrick and Prince, and you'll be in my shop."

We shook hands. Everything was fine, except with the house property man, who said, "No, no! You can't throw me out of my theatre! We get paid! Not only do we get paid for all the hours that Pete was there, but we also get paid for time and a half and turnaround time for the next day!"

The bill was enormous. Technically, he was right. Morally, he was a shit. I walked around town facetiously saying I'm paying 1500 dollars to have him killed and I could get it down to 800 dollars—there were guys willing to do it for less. In the mail, or I forgot how, comes a little note. It says, "Get the payroll for the movie theatre on 45th Street." That's all it says.

I got a hold of that payroll, but I don't remember how. It is a felony to be on two payrolls at the same time if you are a stagehand. Apparently, this house property man was on two payrolls. There's a grievance scheduled at the International ("The IA"), which is the stagehands' union, and the question is, do I have to pay this bill? I am refusing to pay.

The head of the IA at the time was a good guy named Al Di Tolla. I came to the meeting in my suit and when I arrived, Al Di Tolla came over and asked, "Do you have in your pocket what I think you have in your pocket?"

I said, "Yes." It was the payroll from the movie theatre on 45th Street.

He asked, "Would you excuse us?"

And that was the last I heard about anything. The theory is that the IA cannot make a judgement on a felony, otherwise they'd be accessories after the fact because being on two payrolls at the same time was a federal crime. To this day, I have no idea who sent me that note. It was either Frank DeVerna, Pete Feller or Al Di Tolla, all of whom were my trusted friends.

Our general manager was Jose Vega. Jose Vega was an ex-flamenco dancer, and he was knowledgeable and fearless. We did a show once that Herb Gardner wrote called *Thieves*. Herb Gardner was a little nuts, and very demanding. Peter Larkin designed the set and Michael Bennett directed it. The work that Michael Bennett did in musicals was spectacular, but directing plays was, I think, a little out of his league. In any case, the play takes place in two high-rise apartment buildings in New York City. So what the audience saw on the stage was two tall New York City buildings.

We're sitting in the office on 46th Street and Peter Larkin is gonna show us the model of the scenery. Bernie Jacobs, who is head of the Shuberts, comes in with Michael Bennett. Bernie Jacobs was in love with Michael Bennett... I don't mean literally, but Michael could do no wrong.

In any case, we're sitting in the office and Peter Larkin shows us this model with the two towers going up and everyone is saying, "It's gorgeous! It's gorgeous!"

Jose says, "Except nobody in the orchestra after row H is going to be able to see a fucking thing. You don't know what the fuck you're doing!"

Well, it freezes the moment. Then he says, "It's a good thing we're playing seaports in New Haven and Boston because we'll need a ship to transport this set."

Bernie Jacobs says to Jose, "You can't talk to Michael Bennett like that!"

Jose says to Bernie, "And you know less than he does!"

The next five days were spent with the Shuberts wanting to have Jose Vega fired, but of course we never did.

So I had Pete Feller as a set builder and carpenter, Frank DeVerna providing the electrics, and Jose Vega as a general manager, so no stagehands argued with any of them. Even the unions backed off. My life was made very simple. If we wanted to do a play, then we did the play. I did not have to worry about what anything cost regarding the physical show.

Frank would call up and ask, "What do you want to pay?"

And I would say, "I don't know, what is the correct price?"

I always got the correct price, but if the show was in trouble, I could correct it without a big to-do. So given that, I could do six shows on Broadway and shows on the road as well. It was busy and it was classy.

While I was doing all of that, I was also general managing shows for Joe Papp at the New York Shakespeare Festival/The Public Theater. Bernie Gersten, who worked with Joe Papp, was a good friend and sometimes I did the shows for nothing and sometimes I got paid. I general managed the road company of *A Chorus Line* and that's also when I broke up with Gene Wolsk.

The truth was that Michael Bennett didn't want Gene Wolsk as the general manager of the tours. Bernie Gersten and Joe Papp wanted me to be the general manager of *A Chorus Line*, but Michael Bennett and I had disagreements on *Thieves* and *God's Favorite.* We didn't hate each other, but if you don't have a winner, there's a little bit of finger-pointing, so we're all to blame for the outcome. When Michael did *A Chorus Line* on Broadway, we didn't get the call to be the general managers. We didn't care a whole lot about it because we were busy producing by then. When the road companies came up, Bob Kamlot, who was the general manager for the show in New York, really knew nothing about the road, so I did it.

A Chorus Line has gay components, and a lot of young people were beginning to come out. It was a whole new revolution on Broadway. Then came the AIDS epidemic which devastated the community. Kids died. I gave a number of eulogies for young kids. T. Michael Reed, who was the dance captain of *A Chorus Line* and *Cats*, was a nice guy. I gave a eulogy for him at Sardi's, and I was looking at who was there, and I was surrounded by kids. I was fifty years old, and they were twenty years old—they were going to funerals. I blurted out, "Young people should not go to funerals. Old people go to funerals."

It prevailed through the '80s. When we did *Jerome Robbins' Broadway*, one kid was HIV positive. He accidentally fell and cut himself. The room emptied because of the blood. It was terrible. A lot of young people that we knew (and people that we didn't know) died.

In the late 1970s, I really started producing a lot of shows. I did *Chapter Two, I Ought to Be in Pictures,* and in 1978 I produced *Ain't Misbehavin'.* It was originally done at the Manhattan Theatre Club, which was much smaller than it is now. I saw it and said, "Let's do it." It was a relatively empty season for musicals, and it won the Tony. It was up against Bob Fosse's *Dancin'.*

In those days we used to eat dinner at Wally's, a steakhouse on 49th Street. It was a big hangout for showbusiness, and there were kinda camps. There was the *A Chorus Line* camp, which was Michael Bennett, Bernie Jacobs and the Shuberts. Then there was the Fosse camp, which was Sam Cohn, the agent, and of course Fosse, who was the great stylist. He was the better choreographer, if you want to compare things, but he didn't have the big hit. Michael Bennett did. Fosse thought Michael Bennett's choreography was simplistic.

There was an article written in *The New York Times* about how Bernie Jacobs ate at The Polish Tea Room and Sam Cohn ate at The Russian Tea Room. At the end of the big article it said, "...but whenever there was a problem, it was resolved by Manny Azenberg, who walked in between them." My mother was still alive at the time, and she was quoted saying that she was "really proud to know that her son could solve problems between two big mongols." Not moguls, mongols.

I said, "I think you may be right, Ma."

Around this time my father was still alive, and he would often come to the office. It was a big office, and it was my office, and there were a lot of people working there. I think he was always totally supportive of my career, but I wanted him to know that I was okay. There were shows on Broadway, and *Ain't Misbehavin'* had just won a Tony Award, and I think he knew that I was okay.

The Polish Tea Room was run by Harry and Frances Edelstein, Holocaust survivors from Poland. My parents came from Poland, and Harry and Frances knew that part of my family was killed in the Holocaust. I knew a little Yiddish and I was also an unashamed Jew. There was a reserved table up front where a small group of Holocaust survivors would sit and have lunch. Harry would introduce me as Neil Simon's producer and say to them, "Ehr vais," which means, "He knows."

Harry was a really generous man. He had a theory that if you had a cold and you just wanted soup, you shouldn't have to pay for it. Chicken soup is like medicine, and you shouldn't charge for medicine.

I came in one day with you and your sister, Rebecca, and there was a Black man standing beside the front door. He sold knock-off watches from a small suitcase and Harry went over to him and took out two Mickey Mouse watches for you and Rebecca. Later I asked Harry, "What was that all about?" Harry explained that this man would come into The Polish Tea Room, sit at the counter, and only order soup. There was cabbage soup, beef and barley soup, or chicken soup with crackers—it was a very hearty meal. But the guy wouldn't order anything else and Harry, who was a busybody, went over to him and said, "Order some food!"

The guy said, "I can't afford it."

Harry gave an order to his staff that whenever this man, who was an illegal from Uganda, comes into the restaurant, he must be fed.

"He comes in, you feed him. People should not go without food."

So I heard this story, and I went over to Harry and I invoked Jewish tradition. "Your mitzvot, your good deeds, are not mine." You had to talk to Harry in Talmudic terms. I said, "Here's twenty-five dollars. Give it to the guy."

Harry said, "No no no..."

I said, "Your mitzvot are not mine."

Two weeks later, I came into The Polish Tea Room and the guy came over to me and said, "Thank you."

So that was The Polish Tea Room. People think I named it as a counter to The Russian Tea Room, but it was named because Polish Holocaust survivors owned it and hung out there. It's an extraordinary story of two immigrants who survived the camps.

It became a great hangout, and I had my table in the front, which was an exclusive area. Mike Nichols would go there, Neil Simon would go there, the Shuberts would go there, and the stagehands and the chorus kids would go there. On Wednesday afternoons, magicians would be in the back, showing each other magic tricks. You could go to dinner alone and you would end up having dinner with seventeen people that you knew. It was good. It was fun. It was a wonderful coffee shop, and it was a hangout for all of showbusiness.

11 "EVERYWHERE BUT WASHINGTON, SENATOR"

Here comes one of the big stories. One of the great bookings on the road is at the Kennedy Center in Washington, D.C. It was run by a very rich guy who was a big wheel named Roger Stevens. He was responsible for establishing the Kennedy Center and was also the chief fundraiser for the Democratic Party during the '50s when Adlai Stevenson was running against Eisenhower.

You couldn't get a booking there because Roger chose shows that suited his own personal taste. He would go to London and bring over British shows like *Private Lives* and some Somerset Maugham play. When Neil wrote *Chapter Two*, it was a major success on Broadway. It may have been the most financially successful play in its time ever. When it was time to book the road company, we couldn't get into the Kennedy Center, even with a very successful Neil Simon play. I said to Neil, maybe even arrogantly, "Let's make some trouble about the fact that the Kennedy Center is a public building, and we can't get your play in there. You're Neil Simon, an American playwright, and you can't get a booking in that theatre."

In that period of time, the inner cities were dangerous everywhere—New York, Philadelphia, Washington D.C. In fact, when we did *The Sunshine Boys* in Washington D.C., we had limousines waiting at the stage door in order to get out of the neighborhood. You didn't want to walk the streets. Things got so bad in downtown Washington D.C. that the National Theatre had been taken over by Roger Stevens, because he was the only player in town. So he's running the Kennedy Center and the National Theatre.

I got together with Marvin Kraus who was the general manager/producer on *Beatlemania*, and with Jack Schlissel who was the general manager of *The Best Little Whorehouse in Texas*. I said, "Let's take your two shows and my two shows, *Ain't Misbehavin' and Chapter Two*, and play somewhere else."

We found the Warner Theatre, which was two blocks away from the National Theatre. Both were located in the inner city. What Roger Stevens was putting into the National Theatre were Black shows, and it was horrifically referred to as "a nigger house." I wasn't going to cater to Roger Stevens—I just didn't want to be dictated to by him. Also, if you played the National Theatre, the subscription went down to a thousand, as opposed to a subscription of 28,000 at the Kennedy Center. So we booked all four shows at the Warner Theatre.

At this point in time, Senator Bill Bradley is a friend and we helped raise money for his senate campaign. One of my investors, Eli Jacobs, was a heavy-duty Republican from Baltimore who knew all the Republican senators—Howard Baker, Rudy Boschwitz from Minnesota, Alan Simpson from Wyoming, Jacob Javits from New York. He invited all of them to the opening night of *Ain't Misbehavin'* in Washington and they all went to the party afterwards and sat at a table together.

Eli Jacobs asked me in front of all the Republican senators, "Why don't you tell them about the trouble you're having with Roger Stevens, a Democrat?"

The New York senator was Senator Javits, ya know, a Republican. I said, "I have a problem, but Bill Bradley will take care of my side of the aisle."

You know... I'm joking.

Senator Javits said, "You're a New Yorker. I represent you, not Bill Bradley, he's from New Jersey," and everybody laughed.

At the end of the table, Senator Simpson from Wyoming asked,

"You mean to say that I had to sit through that Somerset Maugham shit, and I couldn't see *Ain't Misbehavin'* at the Kennedy Center?" [Dad impersonates him in a somewhat Wyoming accent.]

I said, "That's right, Senator."

He said, "Well you tell Bradley, I'll be the other side of the aisle..."

The Kennedy Center funding comes from Congress, and various committees allocate money. So when this issue came up on the Senate floor, Bill Bradley questioned it, and then Alan Simpson questioned it. They were just two freshman senators. This made the front page of *The Washington Post*, and it became a big thing. It had all sorts of implications. The New Yorkers are trying to tell us what to do... it might even have been that the Jews are trying to tell us what to do. When it was brought up to Roger Stevens that his budget might be held up, he said that he really couldn't be too disturbed by two freshman senators.

Big mistake, because these two senators were formidable, and they were also very tall. It went back and forth, and there was finally a hearing in the Senate. The committee was chaired by Senator Pat Moynihan, who was the other senator from New York. Moynihan didn't allow the press in because this was a real scandal sheet story. The people who showed up complaining were Black dance groups, Neil Simon, and Paddy Chayefsky. These were groups who couldn't play their shows at the Kennedy Center. Bernie Jacobs and Gerry Schoenfeld (the Shuberts) did not want to show up because, frankly, I think they were afraid of Roger Stevens, but Bill Bradley called them up and said, "I do not speak frivolously on the Senate floor. You will be there."

They showed up. There were many people who were afraid to show up. This was a story about the theatre which was occupying the Senate.

Senator Moynihan, who was a friend of Roger Stevens, could talk and he chaired the meeting. He said that when he was the Ambassador to India, his daughter was in a production of Neil Simon's *The Gingerbread Lady*.

He said to Neil, "Your plays are done all over the world."

Neil said, "Yes, everywhere but Washington, Senator."

Paddy Chayefsky, the playwright, got up and made one of the

great rabble-rousing speeches. Have you ever seen the movie *Network*? "I'm not gonna take this anymore! This is my building! This is not a personal building for anybody. They should be doing American plays!"

Well, the place went crazy.

Also, there was only one person who publicly spoke out against us, and that was Joe Papp from The Public Theater. Joe was my friend, and he knew that we were right because he couldn't get his show, *for colored girls who have considered suicide/when the rainbow is enuf,* into the Kennedy Center. As a result of this, I told him to get *A Chorus Line* out of my office by Friday or I'm throwing it out of the window. That ended our relationship. A number of years later Joe called up and apologized and we reconciled. Sadly, he died of cancer a year later.

I was told later that Senator Moynihan told Roger Stevens that he was gonna lose this fight. What was the end result? The end result was that the Shuberts would get the National Theatre so that there would be competition. While we were in this process, Bill Bradley finds out that there are no Black stagehands at the National Theatre or at the Kennedy Center. This is the nation's capital and there is a segregated stagehands' union.

Bradley called up the head of the international stagehands' union and asked, "Is that true?"

The answer was, "Yes, it's true."

Bradley said, "I'll give you six months to integrate it, or in the seventh month I'll do it for you."

Twenty years later I was down at the National Theatre, giving a talk to students who had gone to see *Movin' Out*. There was a Black man waiting in the corner until I finished. He was either the house property man or the house electrician. He waited until all the kids left and he walked over to me and said, "Tell the Senator we remember, thank you." So Bradley integrated the stagehands' union.

Somebody called me on the phone and offered me the management of the National Theatre. I always thought that was a set-up to see if that was my ultimate motivation... but it wasn't. I didn't respond to it. I said no. I wasn't interested. And that was history.

Senator Alan Simpson went after Roger Stevens on a conflict of interest—you can't run the Kennedy Center for your own personal good. Roger Stevens tried to lobby Simpson with some important people from Wyoming, but Simpson didn't respond. Alan Simpson turned out to be a Republican who supported the arts and who is pro-choice. He and Bradley remain friends to this day. That's a true story of stuff that happened.

That takes us to the late '70s and early '80s. I'm very active on Broadway, maybe the most active that I have ever been. I don't know what that really means, you know... but for the most part I'm doing plays—Neil's plays.

Then Neil called up and said, "Marvin Hamlisch and Carole Bayer Sager came over to discuss the possibility of doing a musical."

They were living together, and they were working together.

Neil asked them, "Doesn't that create conflict? You know, you can have a fight and then you have to be personal. How do you do that?"

They started describing it and Neil said, "I can write that story."

I think within five months he wrote *They're Playing Our Song*. I said, "Let's do it!" and we did. Now I'm in the musical business. It was a flimsy little musical and it only had eight people in it. How do you use a chorus in that story? The critics weren't crazy about it, and it was just entertainment. But the public loved it. It was funny and it was endearing. It ran three and a half years and it toured. It was with Lucie Arnaz and Robert Klein. Marvin Hamlisch was a good guy and he loved writing shows. His death was a big loss.

In the meantime, your mother had been working on shows since I think *The Good Doctor* as a stage manager. She volunteered to be a stage manager and then it became a career. She was also the first assistant stage manager on a show called *Cats*. It seems like yesterday, but it was a long time ago.

When we get to the '80s, we'll talk more. The '80s were my heyday. It's when the trilogy opens, *The Real Thing* opens, *Sunday in the Park with George*, and *Master Harold and the Boys*. We win everything. [Speaking to me] You weren't around then. It seems like yesterday, but it wasn't. It was a long time ago.

Some people remember. You bump into people, and they used to say, "Are you any relation to Manny?"

Now you get, "Are you any relation to Karen?" [My older sister.]

The next one is... "Are you any relation to *Jessie*?"

12 "EMANUEL AZENBERG PRESENTS..."

It's the 1980s and I am now the go-to guy. I have a good relationship with the Shuberts and the Nederlanders. These were the big theatre owners, and in those days, they were really competitive. You were either a Shubert man or a Nederlander man and it sounds like a joke, but it was serious. If you had a good show and you went to the wrong store, the other store didn't like you.

I would have lunch with Bernie Jacobs three times a week, and your mother and I would have dinner twice a week with Bernie and Betty Jacobs. Bernie is the one who changed the Shuberts. He had courage, "chutzpah." He understood that he couldn't pick the plays or musicals, but he knew he could pick the jockeys. If Mike Nichols, Tom Stoppard, Michael Bennett or Sondheim was doing a show, then that's the show you bet on.

There were the old-line producers, Bob Whitehead and Alex Cohen, and then there were probably three young producers–Liz McCann, Marvin Kraus, and me. Liz and I both did plays, but I had Neil Simon. If I really didn't have a serious objection about the play, we did the play. With Neil, the percentage rate that he would make it work was high, there was a big Neil Simon audience, and he was a fixer. He could improve it. Remember, Neil owned the Eugene O'Neill Theatre, so we were the show, the royalties and the theatre owner. It made life very simple, and we had no disputes.

Around this time, however, Neil decided to sell the Eugene

O'Neill Theatre, mostly because he didn't like the business of maintaining it.

"There's a leak, Mr. Simon!"

He didn't give a shit about that. At this point Neil had written two plays that were only marginally successful, *I Ought to Be in Pictures* and *Jake's Women. Chapter Two* was a hit, but we come around to 1983 and Neil writes *Brighton Beach Memoirs.* So now we need a theatre, and I gave it to Bernie Jacobs to read.

After reading it, he said, "It's episodic."

Bernie's ability to read a play is...?! The truth is that nobody really knows about a play until it's on the stage. Bernie really thought that Neil was on his way down, so he passed on *Brighton Beach Memoirs.*

I gave it to Jimmy Nederlander Sr. to read and he said, "You got a theatre. Which one do you want?"

End of discussion.

That theatre was the Alvin Theatre which is now the Neil Simon Theatre. We opened it in L.A., and it was a smash. The audience understood what this play was all about—this was everybody's upbringing. This generation grew up with a sense of family and struggle and it didn't matter if you were Jewish, Italian, Kansas... There was the masturbation scene, which was frightening, but everybody got it. Sam Freedman, who wrote for *The New York Times* and teaches journalism at Columbia, said that this was Neil's best play. The only one who didn't like it was Frank Rich of *The New York Times,* who only gave it a mild review. He hoped that there would be a sequel to *Brighton Beach Memoirs*—he said this one isn't good but maybe the next one will be.

The box office went straight up. It dipped a little from the notice but then it continued straight up. It's a show that ran three and a quarter years. It's the tenth or eleventh longest running show in the history of straight plays. I think the longest running plays are *Life with Father* and *Tobacco Road* and I'm not sure if those old plays ran during the summer. Anyhow, *Brighton Beach Memoirs* was a smash. About a year and half later it was still running, and Neil wrote *Biloxi Blues. Biloxi Blues* only ran a year and a half, but Frank Rich raved about it.

Okay... so your mother and I got married in 1984, which was the beginning of my heyday. This was not in a period where it was 300 dollars a ticket, but I made a decent living... enviable. I didn't cheat. I didn't peddle tickets and I didn't do anything like that, but I had six shows on Broadway at the same time: *Whose Life Is It Anyway? The Real Thing*, *They're Playing Our Song*, *Sunday in the Park with George*, *Master Harold and the Boys*, and the two Neil Simon plays. Who remembers? Out of the six shows, four are real hits and two are successes.

It's not like today, where there are multi-trillions of dollars spent and millions of names above the title. You've seen the posters that we have somewhere, "Emanuel Azenberg presents..." In the Broadway Show League championship game "*Brighton Beach Memoirs* plays *The Real George*." I didn't think much of it at the time, but we were *the* place for Broadway. It was normal. I was not so much in the musical world because *They're Playing Our Song* was a rinky dink musical, but it was a success. *Ain't Misbehavin'* was a small musical and it was a better success because we won the Tony for it. It starred Nell Carter, André de Shields, Armelia McQueen, Ken Page, and Charlaine Woodard, and they were all sensational.

It was a very healthy decade. I don't remember.... I didn't think of it as anything special. I was producing plays by Tom Stoppard, Neil Simon and Athol Fugard. Fugard is a well-known South African playwright who wrote about apartheid in South Africa as a white man. It was a dangerous time and he participated in a lot of courageous activities.

One of Athol's beliefs in those days, not anymore, was that he could only write when he was drinking. It's a common writer's issue and Athol would get drunk on one glass of wine, maybe two. He was never mean, but he'd get philosophical, and this happened a few times. It was always a pleasure to go to dinner with him, but you always knew that this was going to happen, so you had to be prepared. Also, he would insist on paying, which I had to be prepared for because I didn't want him to pay. I thought it would be ungracious of me if I let him pay.

So Jose Vega and I were at dinner with him and after two drinks he asked me, "What is the most important word in the English language?"

I said, "Athol, I'm not going to guess because I'll guess wrong and then I'll put up with your abuse for fifteen minutes because I'll guess wrong."

We laughed about that.

He said, "No, no. You have to guess anyway."

I said, "Okay. Love."

He said, "You are the dumbest man in America."

He did ten minutes on me, and I took it and laughed. I said, "Okay. I'm not guessing anymore. What is the most important word in the English language?"

He said, "Forgiveness."

I asked, "You mean in the big sense? In the Jesus sense? 'Forgive them for they know not what they do'."

He said, "Yes."

I asked, "You want me to forgive Eichmann for killing Jews in the Holocaust?"

He said, "I don't expect you to do that, but I expect you to try. The effort alone will make you a better human being."

Then he said, "I'm insisting on paying."

Now, Athol's had two glasses of wine and he had no credit cards. He took all of his money and folded it up into little pieces. So there was Athol, not sober, unfolding a bill, which was folded into sixteen little squares. He unfolded it and it's only a one-dollar bill. He had to fold it back up and put it back in his wallet. Well, if we stayed there, it would have taken twenty-five minutes to pay the bill until he would eventually unfold a twenty-dollar bill. In the meantime, I would throw a credit card at the waiter and then we'd go outside.

He would insist that the hotel was to the right when it really was to the left. So we walked around the block in a complete circle, but first we had to go to the right and all the way around to arrive at the hotel and he'd say, "You see, I told you it was always to the left."

He was a great playwright and a passionate man. He is still alive and lives in Southern California. He came to New York, and we had lunch about four or five years ago when his production of *The Road to Mecca* was being done at the Roundabout Theatre Company. I said to him, "Remember, I was around when you wrote that play,

Athol. I said I would produce it if you didn't direct it."

He said, "No, I want to direct it. Why don't you want me to direct it?"

I said, "Because you don't have a conclusion to that play. All the characters are you. The conflict is the conflict in you, and it's never going to be concluded unless you have another voice yelling at you."

The next day he was interviewed on television by Charlie Rose who asked him, "So you're doing this play at the Roundabout Theatre Company—what is it about?"

He said, "Call my friend Manny Azenberg, he'll tell you."

So I'm kind of proud of my relationship with Athol Fugard. I would have hoped that he would have won the Nobel Prize for Literature, but he didn't, but he's a great playwright.

Next, Neil wrote *Broadway Bound* and we were going to play at the Richard Rodgers Theatre, which is owned by the Nederlanders.

Why? Because the Shuberts said, "*Brighton Beach Memoirs* was episodic."

The set designer goes into the Rodgers and leans up against the wall and his shirt turns black from soot.

He wrote a letter to Neil and me, which said, "Nobody should be playing in that theatre."

It's a legitimate complaint. The Richard Rodgers Theatre was not always in the best of shape. You'd walk up the aisle and you'd stick to the carpet and there were rats.

So I showed the letter to Jimmy Nederlander Sr. and his general manager, Arthur Rubin. Arthur Rubin said, "Those are Shubert rats."

He said that to me because the Imperial Theatre was being refurbished and it was right next door to the Rodgers—so the rats moved from the Imperial to the Rodgers??

I was somewhat forthright in those days, and I said to Arthur Rubin, "Do you hear yourself talking? The rats have a brand on their ass with an 'S' and you can tell?"

Broadway Bound ended up playing at the Broadhurst which is a Shubert theatre. Eventually, Jimmy Nederlander Sr. made the Richard Rodgers Theatre into the best-looking theatre in the city. I think it's the best theatre on Broadway.

Anyway, *Broadway Bound* is a smash. I think it's Neil's best play. We had Jason Alexander and Jonathan Silverman. Matthew Broderick was in the first two plays but then he becomes a genuine star, so he doesn't do the third one. Jerry Orbach played the father, and the mother was played by Linda Lavin who won the Tony, and she was brilliant.

I did twenty-five plays with Neil Simon, which was not simple. Artists and playwrights have whims. When you work with a playwright, you don't tell them what to write. In *Broadway Bound* there's that scene where the mother dances with the son, which may be one of the best scenes that he ever wrote, and it makes the play. Well, that wasn't in the script six weeks before we went into rehearsal. We had a reading of the play and then we went to dinner afterward, and Neil asked, "What did you think?"

All I said was, "I miss the mother in the second act."

Gene Saks, the director, said he didn't like the particular scene with the girlfriend.

Neil said, "Give me two weeks."

In two days, he wrote a scene that you could not have dreamed of. It had to come from the playwright.

On a separate occasion, there was a joke in *God's Favorite* about hemorrhoids. After two weeks this joke was still in the play. I went over to Neil and I asked, "Hemorrhoids?"

He said, "Don't you think I know?! I don't have anything better."

You have to know that. When you say, "This is no good." Well, what will replace it? And until the playwright knows what will replace it... it fills a gap. You have to be able to make those judgments.

At this point, I've been producing on Broadway for twenty-five years because my first show was in 1966. My friend Bernie Gersten, who worked at The Public Theater and at Lincoln Center, would call up and ask, "Would you put this show out on the road for us?"

I also did *Contact* with Susan Stroman on the road. I was more than the general manager because of my experience on the road, which gave me clout and muscle. I intruded in the show.

Stroman accused me of it but in a friendly way. She asked, "Are you giving notes?"

I said, "I will until you show up." She laughed. I saw her just this weekend.

Neil's next play was *Lost in Yonkers.* Everyone expected Neil to disappear from the Broadway scene and here he comes up with a Pulitzer Prize and a Tony-winning play. The cast included Kevin Spacey, Mercedes Ruehl and Irene Worth, who won Tony Awards. It was a big hit, and it was a huge pay-off for Neil who suffered from never being accepted by the literary world. I contended that *Broadway Bound* was better than *Awake and Sing!* which is part of American cultural history. He was accepted by the entertainment world, and he probably defined comedy for this country, along with Lucy and Desi. He really didn't care about winning Tony Awards, but he was genuinely ecstatic about the Pulitzer.

Lost in Yonkers was originally titled *Louie the Gangster,* but it evolved into a play about a woman. If you look carefully at all of Neil Simon's plays, you don't very often see a woman as the main character. *Lost in Yonkers* turned out to be about Bella, who is slightly impaired, and Grandma Kurnitz. I don't have any understanding of where the Bella character came from. Grandma Kurnitz was vaguely based on his mother-in-law, so you can't give him notes on that character. Very often I knew where the motivations came from, or where the characters came from, but Bella was a real creation of his. Remember, there are two boys in a lot of the plays, and that's Neil and his brother, Danny. But Bella came from nowhere.

In the meantime, I'm still the number one boy for the Shuberts. There were all sorts of rumors that "Manny would become the head of the Shuberts," but I never had any intention of doing that, nor would I take it if it were offered. I didn't want to be a realtor. There's a real truth to what I'm telling you now.

I think a combination of things happened to Bernie Jacobs. He became more and more powerful, and he became a little more arrogant. He was never charming, and he was a tough guy. On a trip to London, Bernie had a stroke and he never really recovered from it. He had significant memory loss, but he didn't want to leave his position at the Shubert Organization.

It affects our relationship because Gerry Schoenfeld is dying to take over, but Bernie doesn't want to let go. Phil Smith, my friend and second-in-command at the Shuberts, is in the middle of it because he's a Bernie guy. Bob Wankel, who is today the head of the Shuberts, was a Gerry guy.

Before Bernie Jacobs had the stroke he asked me, "Would you manage *Sarafina* on the road?"

We joked about what he would pay me, and it was minimum, but I said I would do it.

Phil Smith called me on the phone, and you always knew that there was another agenda with him... talk talk talk... "What, Phil?"

At this point in time, after Bernie's stroke, Gerry Schoenfeld is more in charge of the Shuberts, and he doesn't like *Sarafina*. Phil wants to know if I could raise a third of the money for *Sarafina*. I assumed it was on guarantees from the Shubert theatres around the country, so I said yes. That's a quarter of a million dollars, when the whole show would cost three-quarters of a million dollars. I call friends of mine—Wayne Rogers, Matthew Bronfman, and Bob Malina. We would all put up 62,000 dollars.

Two weeks later, the phone rings again and it's Phil. He asked if I would raise 500,000 dollars. I called the Kennedy Center which had just lost a show and I asked if they would take *Sarafina* and they said yes. I called Phil back and I said, "I'll raise half a million dollars but I'm not playing your theatre." The Kennedy Center is competing with the National Theatre, which is Shubert owned.

I got on the phone with Bernie Jacobs, Gerry Schoenfeld and Phil Smith, and I said, "Look what you've asked me to do. You've asked me to go to my friends to raise the money and then you want me to fuck them over by not giving them the best deal."

Bernie said, "We'll guarantee you against loss in Washington."

I said, "Bernie, that ship sailed. If you want it to play in your theatre, then match the offer."

The Kennedy Center deal was such that you were guaranteed to make a profit of a quarter of a million dollars.

Gerry Schoenfeld got on the phone and said, "Well perhaps the Shubert organization...." [Dad imitates Gerry in a deep and low pretentious voice] and I cut him short and said, "Fuck you. You welched."

I had raised all the money for *Sarafina,* and we didn't talk to each other for a long time. I became estranged from the Shuberts and, sadly, from Bernie Jacobs as well.

Now we're into the early '90s. At about that time, I met two young kids—Kevin McCollum and Jeffrey Seller. Whenever we had a show and it was successful, you'd have what we used to call a bus and truck company. Your brother, Josh, is now out on a tour of *Fiddler on the Roof* which is what we would have called a bus and truck. We didn't bother with doing these tours, so we would give them to somebody else to manage and we would take a percentage. The tours played split weeks, they played one-nighters and short engagements.

Kevin McCollum and his partner Rod Cates walked into the office one day—Kevin remembers that I was swinging a baseball bat which intimidated them. They're in their twenties. I am close to sixty and they are the new kids on the scene. I didn't totally trust the old-line bus and truck producers and these kids wanted to do *Lost in Yonkers* across the country. I said, "Okay. Go do it." They got Mercedes McCambridge, who won the Oscar years ago, to play the lead, and *Lost in Yonkers* became "the little show that could." It just never stopped touring.

Kevin and Rod Cates had some dispute. Rod came into the office and said, "I'm splitting up with Kevin, but I'd like to take over the show."

I didn't know what the dispute was about, but I remember there was a line that I used, and I said, "It doesn't work like that. You leave the dance with the girl you came with."

Jeffrey Seller, who had been working for Kevin, became his partner, and Jeffrey recalls that it's how he made a living for two years. In any case, a few years later, they come up with a show called *Rent.* They'd never done anything on Broadway, and they asked if I could make the theatre deal with the Nederlanders. The cast deal was that everybody was hired on a minimum basis and a shared percentage of the profits. For people who understand the theatre rental business it was a legendary deal because there was no theatre rent paid until the show recouped. We've got to give Jimmy Nederlander Sr. credit because it was a really smart financial deal.

The Nederlander Theatre on West 41st Street looked like a slum, but the show was set in a slum.

Jimmy asked, "Is it fair?" and I said, "It's fair."

Jimmy agreed and everybody shook hands. I only bring that up because it's a minor part of my life that translates into having a lifelong relationship with Kevin and Jeffrey. I worked with them on *Rent, In the Heights,* and *Hamilton,* in which I also invested.

Regarding *Hamilton*, I only had very little to do with it. I made the deal for the theatre, and I negotiated Lin-Manuel's acting deal with Andy Jones, the show's general manager, but that show doesn't require anything. I made some suggestions. Some were listened to, and some were not, and even if I'm right, whether it makes two million dollars more, or doesn't make two million dollars more, is somewhat irrelevant. That show is just a tornado. You didn't think you'd have anyone who could compete with Rodgers and Hammerstein, but Lin-Manuel Miranda does. On the other hand, Jeffrey's family benefits from that show and maybe there is something to behaving decently to people. You show up when they're in trouble or when they're needy, and maybe you benefit ten or twenty years later.

13 THE REAL THING

The most important play that I produced or maybe the one that meant the most to me was Tom Stoppard's *The Real Thing*. It's definitely in the top two. I went to London, and I saw it with Roger Rees and Felicity Kendal. The first time I saw it, I truly didn't understand it. I knew that there was something there, but I didn't get it. It's also written by Tom Stoppard, so you're intimidated automatically.

I was doing a lot of stuff with Mike Nichols at the time and Mike said, "Go see it."

I said to him, "I saw it and we're not gonna do it. You can't just direct it, Mike. It's a hit here in London and it belongs to Peter Wood," who was the original director. Also, there were many other producers who were interested in doing it. I didn't think that the Brits spent any money on the production because the physical show looked cheap. It took ages for scene changes. Then Frank Rich from *The New York Times* wrote a bad notice for it, and anyone from America who was interested in bringing it to New York immediately went away. So Mike and I were the only ones still interested.

We ended up doing *The Real Thing* in New York with Jeremy Irons, Glenn Close, Christine Baranski, and Peter Gallagher. I think Mike was at his best because Stoppard was in the room. Stoppard was his peer—two intellectual and talented giants. Mike described himself as a seducer—literally and figuratively. Mike got the actors to be better than they were, even though they were good already, and the actors in those days respected him. They did what he asked and very often what he asked was extraordinary. He got the play to be better than the production in England. He didn't change a word of the play. Part of directing is just pedestrian and if you have enough chutzpah, you can be a director. A few directors, like Mike Nichols and Elia Kazan, actually have a gift to make something extraordinary happen.

Truth be told, Mike understood that play from reading it. He was brilliant. I didn't really understand the play until I saw it performed three or four times and then I went, "Oh... oh." Even though I didn't get it the first time, it still meant something to me if Mike liked a play and Tom Stoppard wrote it. To quote Stoppard, "You have to become an initiate." You have to become an initiate to art and so I became a little more patient with myself and listened. Nothing Stoppard writes is arbitrary. Unlike with some other plays, you have to revisit Stoppard plays. I don't think anybody gets it right away unless maybe you're a genius. I initially wanted to hide in the theatre because I was afraid Tom would ask me what I thought, and I would appear to be stupid. So I hid in the back of the theatre in Boston. One night there was a tap on my shoulder, and it was Tom and he asked, "What do you think?"

I blurted out, "Ten minutes into the second act, I wasn't paying attention. I was looking at the scenery."

He nodded his head and five days later he came over and asked, "Is it better?"

The Real Thing got better and better for me as I began to understand the intricacies of it. I not-so-jokingly say that I got married because of that play. When your mother and I were living together, we were an odd couple. Your mother comes from an island in Puget Sound, and I come from the Bronx. I'm Jewish and she's whatever. There's so much difference between us but unlike now, she made no demands.

My not-so-joking attitude was that I had been married and I never wanted to get divorced again, so if you don't get married again, then you don't get divorced again. I would have had children without being married, but your mother said no. *The Real Thing* is about the complexity of relationships and relative values. You can have situations where nobody is wrong.

Your mother was working on *Cats,* and she turned to me one day and said, "We're getting married."

I remember thinking I have no excuses anymore. *The Real Thing* helped me say yes to that. The play was a big success—I mean a big success—and it won all the Tony Awards and all the other junk that goes with that.

I wanted to do the film of *Rosencrantz and Guildenstern are Dead*. I had produced *The Real Thing* and *Artist Descending a Staircase*, and I love Tom Stoppard, but I don't know anything about how to do films. My good friend the film and TV producer, Michael Brandman, and I got the rights to do the film of *Rosencrantz*. Michael explained to me that we get the money from distributors around the world, and etc... etc... Sean Connery is going to play the Player King. Well, Sean Connery is "007 James Bond" so you can raise a lot of money on that, and Gary Oldman and Tim Roth are Rosencrantz and Guildenstern, so that's a good group.

We're gonna do the film, and at some point, Connery gets *The Hunt for Red October* movie for three or four million dollars. He begs out but he's got a signed contract with us and that's a dilemma. We're already building scenery at this point, so money is being spent.

I wind up going out to California and meeting with the head agent at CAA. I remember telling your mother, the first half-hour was filled with his bullshit, the next half-hour was filled with my bullshit, so there was no room to breathe with everybody bullshitting each other. The end result was that we had spent 400,000 dollars, and I want 400,000 dollars and I want it right away, otherwise we're suing. I said I'm coming back in two weeks, and I want the check.

I came back in two weeks, and I actually got the check.

Another major part of the story is that Richard Dreyfuss said, "I'll play the part."

Dreyfuss was a big star at the time from *Jaws*. Michael Brandman, Stoppard, and I had a meeting. Do we go ahead with it? There's a huge problem. Richard Dreyfuss was worth a million dollars less than Sean Connery to the distributors. This means that the risk is that you're going to ultimately have a million dollars less to work with.

I said, "Let's not do it. It's too big a risk."

Stoppard said, "No. Let's do it. I'll stand for a third of it." Now, he's the author and the director and he has nothing to do with producing the movie, but he said, "I'm going to join you financially."

Michael thought about it and he said, "Okay, let's do it."

I said, "I'm not going to leave the canoe." You know, it's one of my expressions. We shook hands.

The movie was made, and although it won the Venice Film Festival and a few other minor awards, it did not do well at the box office. However, two and a half years later, the bill arrived for the million dollars. The first check was from Tom Stoppard who had said, "I'll stand for a third of it."

Just from a handshake—no lawyers, no agents, no nothing. Class act. My relationship with Stoppard has lasted close to forty years.

14 JEROME ROBBINS' BROADWAY

Did we talk about *Jerome Robbins' Broadway*? Throughout my career I got the reputation that I knew something about dance, which I really didn't. Maybe it's because I was friendly with Jack Cole and that word traveled around. I had managed Twyla Tharp's company on Broadway, worked with Michael Kidd on *The Rothschilds* and now with Jerry Robbins. The truth is, I knew nothing. My career in theatre in dance is an accident, but it's a good one.

In the mid-80s, the idea of doing a compilation of Jerome Robbins' work had been around for a number of years. It was always intriguing because he was Jerry Robbins. I think Robbins' lawyer, Floria Lasky, came to Bernie Jacobs and asked if he was interested in doing it.

Bernie said yes and then asked me, "Would you do it?"

I said, "Sure," because I knew that Jerry Robbins was a genius. He had a difficult reputation, but I thought that with me he'd be wonderful... Maybe I was a bit arrogant...

Well... I spent most of my time protecting the dancers from him. If one girl gained two pounds, then she was put in the back of the line. He was cruel. In effect, the dancers and I shared a mutual enemy. He wasn't cruel to everybody. He was okay with Jason Alexander and Scott Wise. Charlotte d'Amboise was okay too because she's a d'Amboise, but the more vulnerable ones needed protection.

He even ran afoul of George Balanchine who evidently told him, "If you're not happy at the New York City Ballet, you can leave."

Everybody agreed that he was a cruel person, and everybody had theories about his anger—he didn't want to be Jewish, he didn't want to be gay, whatever it was. It actually seemed so unnecessary. He was a handsome man with a big smile and an enormous talent.

The rehearsals for *Jerome Robbins' Broadway* were at the 890 Broadway Studios. I brought a photo into rehearsal one day of you and your sister, Rebecca, when you were little. I was showing it to the dance captains and Jerry Robbins walked in and he asked, "What are you guys looking at?"

Somebody said, "We're looking at a photo of Manny's kids."

Jerry looked at the photo, and I mean he *really* looked at it and he was serious. He said, "It must give you a lot of pleasure."

I think it was an indicative line. I think that photo represented what he didn't have. He had a dog, but it was 1988 and he wasn't going to have children. I think it was an interesting moment and it was a calm one. He was not his normal antagonistic self. Maybe it was all those issues that made him a genius....

I made my only real contribution to *Jerome Robbins' Broadway* when I went to meetings at his house. He would outline the show, and in every meeting, *Peter Pan* was missing. He never mentioned it in the first meeting, the second meeting, etc... Finally, I said, "Let's put *Peter Pan* in the show."

He aggressively asked, "Why?!"

By this time, I knew that I couldn't take him on directly. I told him, "One, *Peter Pan* is great for kids—kids love to see *Peter Pan*. Secondly, it's got a great look because they fly. And thirdly, nobody knows you did it, Jerry."

That last point was my clever bit. All of a sudden *Peter Pan* was in the show and Charlotte D'Amboise played that part. Remember when I'd show up with you and Rebecca and we would visit Charlotte backstage? You thought that Charlotte was Peter Pan. She had magic dust and she sprinkled it on top of you. That was a highlight.

None of the creators wanted to give Jerry the rights to their shows. No one liked him. It was Leonard Bernstein who convinced everybody that it was okay. It was in that year that Leonard Bernstein turned seventy. There was a celebration for him in Vienna, Berlin, London, Paris, and New York. Jerry Robbins turned seventy that year and nobody gave a shit. We rehearsed for six months, and the rehearsals were endless. I don't know what his process was. Maybe he was just getting old or maybe he was hesitant, but other people had to come in and remind him what the steps were. He just didn't remember.

Later on in the process we knew we had to make cuts. The obvious cut was a section from *On the Town*, composed by Leonard Bernstein. The one guy that Robbins didn't want to insult was Bernstein. Jerry asked him to come and see the show and presumably cut a certain section of *On the Town*. So Bernstein came to see it.

Bernstein was dying, literally. He was smoking. He had an inhalator in one hand and a cigarette in the other. He was very hunched over and diminished in stature. We had met previously socially, and he came over to me and said, "You don't look so bad."

I didn't refer to him as Lenny. I said, "Mr. Bernstein, I used to be 6'4" ...

Bernstein was hunched over, and he said, "Look at me! I did three, *three* shows with him."

Bernstein told Robbins to cut the *Fiddler on the Roof* section—he didn't want to cut a number from his own show. Ultimately, we cut some of *On the Town* and also a piece from *Fiddler on the Roof*. You have the rehearsal piano played by Leonard Bernstein in your apartment. Your brother, Josh, the famous musician, has also played on that piano.

There were many instances of difficulty, so much so that I think after six months, I said, "I quit!"

He was too aggravating, too difficult. He wrote me a letter asking me not to quit and I don't know what ever happened to that letter. I should have kept it somewhere. I just couldn't deal with him anymore. He was too irrational.

He lived on 84th Street and he decided that he needed a hotel room right next to the theatre, so we gave it to him. He would order up food for himself and the dance captains. When we told him that it was getting too expensive, he made the dance captains pay for their own food. I don't think he was a generous person. The saving grace was that he did take care of a lot of kids with AIDS, so you gotta give him credit for that.

There were sixty-two dancers in that show. That's a lot of people. And then some left, and there were replacements, and then there was the road company. There probably were a hundred people who performed in that show, and they would describe it as the highlight of their dance career. It's not a legendary show, but it's legendary for the people who were in it. It was only excerpts from his shows, but for those who know, the twenty-five-minute ballet of *West Side Story* will never be done as well. Those were the best Broadway dancers at that time and maybe even now. When New York City Ballet does it, it's a little... dainty.

Jerome Robbins' Broadway was done at the Imperial Theatre, and the next show that went in there was *Les Misérables.* Scott Wise, a dancer in *Jerome Robbins' Broadway,* went to the carpenter for *Les Miz* and asked that when the show closes and you take out both decks, please cut out a piece of the Robbins' deck and give it to me. I think that for all of those dancers it was... if you were one of the sixty-two dancers in that show, then you had made the big leagues.

Jerry did not like the title *Jerome Robbins' Broadway*, so he put up a chalkboard in the rehearsal room for suggestions for a new title. Jerry's real last name is not Robbins, it's Rabinowitz. One morning, I walked in, and I saw the chalkboard and I wrote down my suggestion, which was, "Dancin' Hits by Rabinowitz."

Jerry Mitchell, who was one of the dance captains, asked me, "Are you really gonna leave that up there?"

I said, "Yes, I am."

A little while later, Robbins walked in and read it and yelled, "Who wrote that?!"

I said, "I wrote that."

Jerry asked, "What do you mean 'Dancin' Hits by Rabinowitz?"

I asked, "You know how many theatre parties I could sell with the name Rabinowitz?"

So that's Jerry Robbins. *Jerome Robbins' Broadway* was the single best and worst experience of my life. It's now anecdotal so I can look back on doing a musical with Jerry Robbins. Everything about Robbins' ballets and about the shows he created is extraordinarily humanistic. Except him—he's not. Everybody says that he was a terror, including Hal Prince, Stephen Sondheim, Leonard Bernstein, and many others. There were times when it was an excruciating experience. We rehearsed for six months, six days a week, with sixty-two dancers, and he was cruel. It's like a number on your arm, except it isn't terrible, but it is a number on your arm.

However, when you see the end result of his work either at the New York City Ballet or on the Broadway stage, it's breathtaking. Just look at the choreography for *West Side Story*, the bottle dance in *Fiddler on the Roof*, or the opening number in *A Funny Thing Happened on the Way to the Forum*. He created that. As much as I complain about Robbins or Neil Simon or Tom Stoppard, and I don't complain too much about Neil Simon and Tom Stoppard, I was in the room with them. I was the producer of *Jerome Robbins' Broadway*, and I was "in the room where it happened." I don't know if the industry will ever have somebody like Robbins again, but it's a show that will go on the resumé of my soul and it's the best you can hope for as a producer.

15 LICENSE TO DO OTHER THINGS

My success in the theatre business gave me license to do other things. I taught a theatre course at Duke University for twenty years, and I hosted over thirty trips to Israel. These two experiences enriched my life in other ways. I was never fixated only on the theatre business, which can be obsessive and limiting. You have to expand your interests because it adds a dimension to your life.

In the early 1980s, producers went up to Yale to see plays for a possible transfer to Broadway. I was asked to guest teach a class for Yale's graduate theatre school. I was somewhat intimidated by Yale and Harvard. I gave the students in my class a new play that I was going to produce on Broadway called *Brighton Beach Memoirs*. The responses from the students were almost to the person negative.

One student came up to me after class and said she really liked the play but was afraid to admit it because it was written by Neil Simon—it wasn't Strindberg, Ibsen, or Chekov. Apparently at Yale, Neil Simon was known as just a pedestrian writer. There were three professors at Yale that had come from journalism and academia. They were Stanley Kauffmann who murdered *The Lion in Winter*, Robert Brustein, and Richard Gilman, both of whom are well-known and harsh critics. The people, like me, who were invited to talk to the students were much more practical participants in the professional theatre. *Brighton Beach Memoirs* had not opened yet, but when it came into New York it was a huge success.

I went back up to Yale and said to the students, "I guess you are not the most intelligent people in America because, very frankly, you've just pissed all over the most successful comedy in two decades. Most of you would like to be me, and the truth is, I don't even think your opinion of the play is your own personal opinion. I think you are giving me back the opinion of your teachers, which is an elitist opinion, and the danger with that is that you are going to have to maintain that for the rest of your life. If you begin to fake who you really are, then you become those people that we don't really like. You're posturing rather than having an opinion. I know this because there are one or two of you who admitted that they liked the play but were literally afraid to say so."

It was from that experience that I created my class at Duke University. Your sister, Lisa, went to Duke and I went down to visit her—the Duke campus is gorgeous.

I don't know who it was, but somebody asked me, "Would you like to teach here?"

Good intuition is where you say yes to something and you don't know the outcome, but you have a shot that it might become meaningful. The intention of my class was to respect the idea that there can be more than one opinion, and not to be intimidated by somebody who you think is more intelligent than you. If the smartest people in the room like Beethoven, and you don't like Beethoven, you feel stupid. Well, no, you shouldn't. I would give them plays to read and I'd rip the cover off the script, and I begged them not to look up anything on the internet. I demanded that the students have their own opinion and told them that it was okay to not like the play because the art world is subjective. The students read thirty plays in a semester, and the papers that they wrote had to be visceral responses.

I had a student who was a wrestler. He technically should not have taken the course, but it was fine because the course was about having an opinion. The more complicated plays were too difficult for him, but he could read Neil Simon and have a good time.

His father came to the last class and said to me afterwards, "This is the only class in which my son's opinion was respected." It was very moving.

Other than having to get up very early on Thursday mornings and fly down to North Carolina, it turned out to be okay. It was something I really looked forward to. I actually developed a course to teach that was completely my own. There was no posturing, or there was very little posturing. When you teach, you're posturing a little bit, but it was the one place where I was the most honest that I could be. I learned from my students.

I think there may have been one kid in twenty-five years at Duke who actually understood *The Real Thing* from reading it. Fifteen years later they'd call me up and say, "I get it now."

The kids were for the most part smarter than I was, but I knew what the plays were about, so I had an advantage. I was also better able to bridge generational issues because of that and it became a very popular course. I enjoyed teaching at Duke University more than I enjoyed the Broadway thing.

Thirty-five years ago, Woody Allen wrote an article in *The New York Times* condemning Israel during the second Intifada, the Arab–Israeli guerilla war.

When asked if he had been to Israel he said, "Why should I go to Israel when I can go to Sweden?" He was implying that the Swedish women were better looking than the Israeli women.

That article was the original impetus for the trips to Israel. I started taking people there just to shatter their preconceptions of Jews and Arabs—the Arabs don't look like terrorists and the Jews don't all look like the Hasidim. There is an existence of self-loathing in the Jews of my generation. Your Jewish identity is conflicted with your American identity. I can only acknowledge that up to a point.

When we were little, a kid on the street would come up to you and ask, "If there was a war between Israel and the United States, who would you fight for?"

The answer was "the United States" and that would stop the argument. But there was antisemitism in the street, and obviously there was antisemitism in Europe.

You can help shatter the preconceptions that Jews have of Jews by bringing them to Israel. Israel is an assemblage of people from all over the world, and you meet people whose parents came from Iraq, and Iran, and Russia, ya know, everywhere, even Ethiopia. The trip is a revelation and an education for both Jews and non-Jews. People realize that Israel is a complicated place and things are not so simple. We meet the right wing, the left wing, Arabs and Jews... We mostly took people from the theatre, some very well known, some not, some students and some complete strangers. For the most part, there was no proselytizing and no politicking. The politics and the religious issues are built into the country, and you can draw your own conclusions from them. You also got the sense of what the Holocaust really meant.

I think that more than six hundred people have gone on the trip over the years. Our tour guide for the first trip was a guy named Ron Perry. He was randomly hired by the Anti-Defamation League, who sponsored the first couple of trips, and for thirty years he's the only guide we use. He is a human encyclopedia and he's an ardent Zionist, and an atheist, so he's an education unto himself. In the theatre business, everybody knows about the trip and people want to go. Also, your mother did all of the work to arrange those trips every year. So she must have organized more than six hundred people over the last thirty-five years.

Mary Rodgers, Richard Rodgers' daughter, went on the trip three or four times. On her first trip, we met two Ethiopian teenagers who had just come to Israel as part of Operation Solomon, and they were being oriented into Israeli society. We met a fifteen-year-old kid who we called George (his name wasn't really George) and he had this gorgeous smile. We asked him in English, after coming from the mountains of Ethiopia to Israel, what has been the biggest culture shock? The question and answer were translated into Hebrew, and then from Hebrew into Aramaic, and back again. He responded with this big smile on his face and said that he never knew that there were white Jews, which stunned everybody, especially Mary Rodgers.

Then we asked the girl the same question and she spoke a little English.

She said, "When we were little children in the mountains of Ethiopia, we were always told that there was a Garden of Eden—and we're here."

Mary Rodgers froze. She was absolutely stupefied and stunned by the presence of these Jewish Black teenagers and the continuity they represented. As a result of those trips, she helped start a Broadway musical theatre program with Jane Summerhays at Tel Aviv University. So that was nice. The point is that those Israel trips impacted people's awareness.

My father was a definitive Zionist, and I don't say that lightly. He dedicated himself to creating a homeland for the Jews. Israel became a state in 1948 and I remember sitting in the kitchen with my father as he checked off each country that voted for Israel's existence. When the United States voted, that was it. The resolution passed in the United Nations and my father said, "It happened in my lifetime."

My father was in his fifties by then, and although he visited Israel, he never made Aliyah. Many years later at your sister Lisa's Bat Mitzvah, he pounded on the table and said, "Quiet."

He said that throughout his whole life he was searching for a "raison d'être," a reason for life. He had witnessed that day a Bat Mitzvah ceremony for his granddaughter in a reform synagogue, and the idea of celebrating a Bat Mitzvah at Sardi's in the theatre district was unheard of. He said that he realized that whatever his tradition was, it would be continued in ways he could not possibly have imagined. There's a word for this in Hebrew, "Hemshech," which means continuity. Everybody was crying by the end of his speech...

So over the years, we have made this trip to Israel thirty times. On the last trip to Israel, we took Jeffrey Seller and Josh Lehrer and their children with us. Jeffrey and Josh are good friends of mine, and they contributed a substantial amount of money to the Khan Theatre in Jerusalem, a theatre that has both Arab and Jewish actors. A part of that deal was that the courtyard of this theatre would be named in honor of Lani and Manny Azenberg for their Israel trips. You know, your mother is not Jewish, she grew up in Seattle, so ultimately the dream of her life was not exactly that there would be a courtyard named after her in Jerusalem! [Dad being funny...] but she was very pleased and grateful to be included.

When we were there last year, my father would have been 125 years old. His name, "Azenberg," is etched on that stone, so he finally made Aliyah at the age of 125. The stone represents something permanent, and we live through our children, so it's okay. He knew that his identity would be continued in ways that he could not possibly have imagined.

16 SUMMING UP...

One of the realities is that the theatre is a transient business but there were many good social times too. There were lots of good actors, designers, directors, and writers that I worked with. People like Zeljko Ivanek and Joyce Van Patten are good people. Robert Preston, Glenn Close, Peter Gallagher, I'm trying to think of.... Danny Glover, when we did *Master Harold and the Boys*, he's a class guy.

[Speaking to me] Was it you that went to see Danny Glover in *Master Harold and The Boys*? Yes, I remember, you said to me, "You know Danny Glover?!"

John Ritter was a really nice guy and Henry Winkler too. In almost all of the Neil Simon plays, the understudy was Dick Latessa who just died recently. He was a regular Neil Simon actor who understood the rhythms in Neil's lines. Nathan Lane was a consummate professional. He came prepared. He was ready. He took it seriously. I like him personally and I respect him in a big-league way, and I respect his approach to the theatre.

Tharon Musser was one of the great lighting designers. She was an artist and I liked her. We did forty-two shows together. To say I trusted her would be one of the great understatements.

We had a relationship where we never negotiated her contract. She would bring the union contract into my office, put it on my desk, and say, "Fill it out." It was never negotiated, and she simply got what the scenic designer got. I was never going to give her less, even if the scenic designer was more important.

I only did one or two shows with Bob Crowley, and he is a genius. I did a lot of shows with John Lee Beatty whom I really liked. The trick with the designers is, do you trust them? They will tell you one thing and then come up with something else, and then you will get a bill for half a million dollars. I didn't have too much of that with them. They were artists and there's that trust thing, you can't underestimate it.

I did *The Lion in Winter* with Jimmy Goldman who was a class act. Fugard should have won the Nobel Prize. Neil Simon was difficult, but he was more about the theatre than almost anybody I've ever known. He loved it. He loved writing the plays. He loved actually writing. He loved the rehearsal process and the previews and then it's over and he's on to the next one. I think he deserves some defense against the literary critics, if for no other reason than he had thirty years of success. He had seventeen major hits, twenty-two successes, something like that, and nobody has taken his place. If you can make a country laugh, then you've... As some famous somebody once said, "Comedy is a lot harder than drama."

There are one or two people that I invested in with friendship, and I was disappointed that it didn't continue—Hal Holbrook was one and Bob Loggia was another. I was friends with Hal's first wife and his second wife, and then twenty years later you're not. You're almost strangers. Time, distance, and other shows separate you.

I also produced the show *Movin' Out*. I didn't get along with Twyla Tharp, the director/choreographer. When we tried out *Movin' Out* in Chicago, it was missing an opening number. In a conversation with Twyla, I invoked Jerry Robbins' opening numbers. *Fiddler on the Roof* has "Tradition," *West Side Story* has the "Prologue," *A Funny Thing Happened on the Way to the Forum* has "Comedy Tonight," so Robbins always sent a message in the beginning of the show to the audience that this is what you're going to see. You're not going to see tragedy; you're going to see "Comedy Tonight!" Or you're going to see a dance show, or you're going to see a show about tradition. It lets the audience off the hook. They can take a breath and go, "Oh, oh okay." Neil Simon would do the same thing. He said I have to make them laugh early, so that they can relax.

Well, we didn't have that in *Movin' Out*. So when I went to Twyla to say we don't have an opening number and I invoked Jerry Robbins, she said to me, "I spoke to him."

There was a big pause because Jerry had been dead for ten years. I asked, "You spoke to Jerry Robbins?"

She said, "Yes."

I knew we were going to have some difficulty because she said she spoke to dead people.

Ultimately Santo Loquasto, the set and costume designer, suggested to Twyla that she introduce the four major characters using "It's Still Rock and Roll to Me" as the opening number. She wasn't going to take a note from me, but she would take a note from Santo Loquasto, and it worked. I paid attention to that show, and it ran for three years in New York and three years on the road. It was old school but there was an audience for stuff like that—there was certainly a Billy Joel audience. I really liked that show.

The two people that I have met in my career who are the most impressive are Tom Stoppard and Bill Bradley. They are driven to be well behaved when no one is watching. The other genius that I worked with, it's gotta be Jerry Robbins, but he was beyond belief badly behaved. However, what was on the stage was spectacular, both in the theatre and in the ballet. I just recently saw *Other Dances* at New York City Ballet, which was a ballet he did for Baryshnikov and Makarova. It's gorgeous.

Michael Kidd, I loved. He was my friend. Jack Cole introduced me to what dance was. I liked him. I suspect that Mike Nichols and Elia Kazan are the two great American directors of the twentieth century for plays. I liked the British director, Howard Davies. He was stubborn and difficult, but I always thought that he chose material that he knew how to do. He taught me what a director should be.

I remember having a meeting with him, I don't know if I told you this, when we did *Private Lives*. Howard said something that really resonated with me. He said, "I know how to do this!"

He wanted to do it because he had an idea about how to do it. He would not do a play just because somebody offered it to him, or his agent called, or there was money to be made.

I thought David Merrick was an evil man, probably pathological, but he had taste. I had a genuinely good partner in Gene Wolsk, he was a good man. And despite having problems at the end of my friendship with Bernie Jacobs, I liked him. I'm trying to think of other people. Biff Liff was a production stage manager at the Merrick office, and we were friends. We worked on the road company of *Oliver!* together. Then he became an agent and we never really wanted to go through a nasty negotiation.

The relationship between producers and agents is mostly a difficult one because you have to negotiate with each other. The agent represents the client, and I represent the show. I say, "10 dollars," and he says, "Screw you, I want a million." You pretend to be friendly but you're not.

We always knew that there was a fair number that we were going to get to. Biff didn't have to prove to the client that he was doing a good job for them because he had a solid reputation. He represented people like Chita Rivera and Angela Lansbury, ya know, big-time people. So we would have lunch where we would agree to write down on our napkins what was a genuinely fair and correct deal. It was called the "Napkin Ceremony."

We had one moment where we hit the number perfectly and we thought that was terrific. We just exchanged napkins. So we attached the napkins to the Equity contract, and Equity kept sending it back because it had napkins attached to it. We would say this is "Exhibit A" and "Exhibit B." It wasn't like that all the time, but we were always close because we had agreed to be fair. Nobody got short-changed. I didn't win, he didn't win, we got to what the correct number was. You couldn't do that with everybody, but I could do that with Biff, and we remained friends until he died.

When Joe Nederlander was young, there was nobody nicer. Everybody loved Joe, and he took care of a lot of people who were down and out. Joe is such a good guy that if we didn't agree on the terms of the negotiation, instead of arguing about it, one of us said, "Let's play tennis for the extra half a point."

We both contended that we could beat each other's ass in tennis.

[Speaking to me, jokingly] I won't tell you who won unless you ask me! That's the way those problems were solved. I think I estimated at one point with the Nederlander family, I must have produced and general-managed forty-two Broadway shows and tours. I don't think there was a contract, it was all on a handshake. The expression I always use is "Who do you want in the foxhole?" I would take Jimmy Nederlander Sr. and Joe in the foxhole at any time. We did business for fifty-five years, ya know. We could yell and scream at each other, but at the end of the day everybody's back was always covered.

17 "HAPPINESS IS...EQUILIBRIUM. SHIFT YOUR WEIGHT."

I don't remember what else I did in the '90s. [I say "*Side Show*" because it is one of my favorites.] Yeah... *Side Show.* I went to a presentation of the show, and I remember looking at the program that was sitting on my chair. I saw that it was about Siamese twins and I said, "Oh God, what am I doing here? A musical about Siamese twins?!" Then I heard the music, and it was wonderful. It was one of those shows that you got involved with because it was emotional, and whoever saw it loved it. I think everyone who was involved in the show would tell you that it was one of the great experiences of their lives.

It was in the same year that *The Lion King* and *Ragtime* opened so it got lost. It ran about three months, and we lost a fortune of money. I think I owed 300,000 dollars after it closed and it took me two years to pay it off, mostly to Serino Coyne, the advertising agency, but every debt was paid off. Alice Ripley played one of the Siamese twins, and she would work the TKTS discount line on 47th Street even when it rained.

When Norm Lewis auditioned, nobody had ever heard of him. Henry Krieger, the composer, and Bobby Longbottom, the director, called me and told me to come down right away to watch an audition for the role of "Jake." Norm Lewis sang and read, and I said, "Well, offer him the part." Nobody did that. You know, you call the agent, and you go through all that crap, so I went up to him and asked, "Would you like to play the part?" and Norm Lewis cried.

The closing night was one of those great theatrical evenings. The cast walked on the stage, and I think the audience must have applauded for eleven minutes. And we just... [I say I remember that evening very well because it was emotional for me too, even at eleven years old.]

But that decade was the beginning of the end of my career. When *Rent* came along, everybody was talking about *Rent Rent Rent*, and I went to see the show with your sister, Karen. To me, it was contemporary music and I actually turned to Karen, and I asked, "Is this good?"

She said, "It's good," and I said "Okay, it's good."

That was the beginning of me starting to deal with generational issues. Along comes all this new stuff, but as Tom Stoppard would say, "It were ever thus."

I had fifteen to twenty years of what I thought was good, and I think that 60% of the shows that I produced were successful. Most of Neil's plays were successful but after *Lost in Yonkers,* Neil began to diminish. We did have some success with *The Dinner Party,* mostly because of the cast that included John Ritter and Henry Winkler. I was still active on Broadway, but I think it's true about producers the same way it's true about artists—they have productive periods when they're attuned to contemporary taste, and then along comes another generation. You might even have success but it's more of an accident rather than you're committed to something.

Then we get to the last year when I'm gonna revive a show that I really like, *Brighton Beach Memoirs.* By this time, Neil was fading. It's now five years later and you know he has Alzheimer's, and he was difficult. I thought it was the best production of *Brighton Beach Memoirs* ever. And God bless them, Nancy and Ellen Simon came to New York to see it and told Neil it was a great production. He wrote letters of apology for all of his complaining. We were gonna do *Brighton Beach Memoirs* and *Broadway Bound* in repertoire, but the audience just didn't show up. I still think objectively that it was a first-rate production, and it actually got decent notices and Neil Simon normally doesn't get good reviews. But the show closed, and we had lost a lot of money—not only my money, but my investors' money.

The same year we lost a fortune of money on the revival of *Ragtime*, which I also think was a first-rate production. That's when—one way or the other—I had to conclude that if this is what I like and it doesn't work, then it may be time to stop, and I stopped. I only have a little bit of petty envy for being active in the theatre. I don't have a lot. I really think that, if you add up all of the plays and all of the shows, you'll come to arguably between sixty-five and seventy shows that I produced, and if you add in the shows that I managed, it comes to about 160. I don't know if anybody could have had a better career.

About six weeks after I closed those shows, I was in Jimmy Nederlander Sr.'s office, who at the time must have been ninety years old. He was in a wheelchair after having had a stroke. He looked at me and he said in that high Nederlander speaking voice, "You lost a lot of money, didn't you?!" [Dad imitates the Nederlander voice.]

I mumbled, "Yeah..."

He said, "Well, I'm paying for half of it."

I said, "Jimmy, I'm a big boy you don't have to do that."

He shook his head and he said, "No, no. That's what friends are for."

It's a telling statement. "That's what friends are for."

Jimmy Nederlander Sr. had made a lot of money on the shows that I did. Nobody had asked for anything. It was normal. I was always treated well. It's a comfortable relationship with the Nederlander brothers, Jimmy Jr. and Nick Scandalios. It transcended the normal disagreements producers have with theatre owners.

I always thought that the understanding of the economics of the show was my responsibility as a general manager as well as producer. If you've made a mistake in selecting a play or a musical that isn't good, at some point you have to deal with the fact that it's not going to be a home run. It's a very rare situation that a producer can take a show that is going to fail and make it into one that is going to be successful. Sometimes you can get lucky with a cast change, like Hinton Battle in *The Wiz*, but you make an aesthetic judgement when you choose the show that you are going to produce.

I chose to do *The Real Thing*. I didn't choose to do *Moose Murders*. If you do three or four *Moose Murders*, you should go into another business. I chose to produce *Devour the Snow*, which closed in a minute, but it was about a real part of American history. *The Poison Tree*, which nobody remembers, is about Blacks in prison, and *Einstein and the Polar Bear* spoke to me—it was about loneliness. There are shows like *Side Show*, the revival that I did of *Ragtime* and *Brighton Beach Memoirs*, that I think should have been successful. You give a little, and you get a little. For the most part, I don't regret the failures. One of the things that happens as a producer in this business, whether a show is successful or not, is that you ultimately wind up respected for the kind of job that you did, and I benefited from that.

There are a couple of shows that I do regret doing and I did them because other people thought they were good. I said, "Well, they must know better than I do." I shouldn't have done *Little Me*, the musical. I should not have done... I forgot the name... John Lithgow was in it... *Division Street*... it was a show that came from the coast, and I think there's one other. Once or twice, I traded off my brain, my soul, and produced shows for what I thought would be money. But it didn't work out. Ever.

I think that, along with the generation gap in taste, the theatre is much different now. Maybe that's the case forever, but the theatre today is much more of a theme park—*King Kong, SpongeBob SquarePants, Charlie and the Chocolate Factory* are different than uh... Neil has a line in a play, I think I told you, the grandfather turns to the kids and says, "You're gonna write? Then it's got to be about something."

Well, the theatre is supposed to be *about* something—something political, social, or moral. Stoppard went into the theatre because it was the "matrix of his moral sensibility." You went to the theatre instead of going to church or to a synagogue. You got your morality from the theatre through the art of that medium. I think it's less so now. Somehow the plays used to be about bigger things. I think we're living in a time when money has suppressed the required art of the theatre. I don't think that off-Broadway shows or not-for-profit shows pick up the slack. The artists have to make a living, and if they don't make a living then they go where they can, which is television and film. The young writers are ultimately in California writing for cable TV.

When I did the play *Devour the Snow*, it failed. It opened on Thursday, and it closed on Saturday. There were a lot of young people in the cast. The notices came out, and they weren't very good—except for John Simon who loved it. I went around being the older guy, comforting all of these young people about their careers, and not to worry and life goes on, etc... and at some point, there was nobody there to comfort me, but there was. There were my two older daughters, Karen and Lisa. When everybody left the opening night party (when you don't get good notices, the party ends quickly), I just walked home with the two of them. Somehow that was more important than the play. I think that was the year that I had four losers in a row, which humbles you. I had begun to think that if I produced it, it would be successful.

There's a line in Stoppard's *The Real Thing* when the daughter turns to the father and asks, "What is happiness?"

The father says, "Happiness is...equilibrium. Shift your weight."

You can interpret that any way you want, but it's about the equilibrium, the balance...

My Broadway career allowed me to teach at Duke University and it allowed me to go on the trips to Israel. If I didn't have those two experiences, as well as my children and my family, then the theatre would be unimportant. I don't want to say that having both a professional and a personal life is key, but it's important. I can't say that I've done it all, but ya know, I'm eighty-six and I am not frustrated about what might have been. The theatre career was fine and exciting, but the Israel trips, teaching at Duke, and my family are all more important parts of my life. I also think gardening is good, and tennis and softball are good.

When asked what am I most proud of? I say my five children (it's like Tevye, "Five!") and four grandchildren. I love the children and grandchildren equally—most of the time. For the record, I was married to Elinor Shanbaum for sixteen years and I've been married to Lani Sundsten for the past thirty-seven years. I don't deserve either one of them. I regret the divorce as a genuine failure—shows just close—but my five children win the Tony every year and Lani is the first person in my "foxhole."

Listen, philosophically, I have no complaints, what can I say? Did I plan any of this? Not at all. None of my life was by intention—this all just happened. Your mother says that she did everything intuitively—good intuition. I did not have an ambition to be a producer. One thing led to another. I was a company manager, and being the company manager led to being a general manager, and then the general managing led to someone asking, "Why don't you produce it?" And then there you are.

There was something that I think I had, in addition to the knowledge of the business—a sensibility about the theatre. When I saw something that was really good, it got to me. I didn't think much of it at the time—I thought it was normal to see *Death of a Salesman* or *Hamilton* and cry. I think that having that sensitivity or sensibility is separate from creativity and is a necessary requirement. I don't think that being a producer is a great thing. I think being a good manager requires a certain ability and is a specific job. In today's world, you can be a producer on a show and get your name up there by just having a lot of money. Genuine satisfaction for a producer is achieved partly from that sensibility that I just talked about.

The other part is to understand how the game is played, the economics of it. It sounds pedestrian, the actual business of the theatre, but you have to understand it—to know what's important. So whether the dresser gets an extra 20 dollars may not seem important, but there are larger economic concepts involved, regarding unions, theatre owners, etc... You and your investors should not be cheated because of a lack of this knowledge. You need to feel comfortable with the people who give you the money.

To find an equilibrium between the artist and the economics is tricky, and it varies from show to show. A producer creates an atmosphere, or tries to, that is genuinely comfortable, so the best creative work can take place. You try to keep peace because there are so many disparate groups within the theatre. I suppose I was good at producing and, since I'm really old now, I'm grateful to have been around in the heyday of Broadway. When you start summing up your life, and your ambition was to go into the theatre, it was a questionable ambition. I just wanted to work in the theatre and to wind up with a reasonably successful career. I think I achieved that and I'm grateful. I don't know if there's a conclusion—it's just an American story. So that's showbusiness. And that's enough for today.

18 LEOPOLDSTADT

Tom Stoppard and I have remained friends for forty years—we did two plays and a film together. I think over the years, very diplomatically, I would kid him about being Jewish and I'd ask him if he would go on the Israel trip. I told him that the difference between being an American and a Brit is that in the United States you can be an Italian American, an Irish American, a Swedish American, an African American, a Jewish American... I said you can't be an Italian Englishman. In order to be an Englishman, you have to give up every other identity. To be a real Englishman, you have to be an Anglo or Celt—everyone else is an immigrant.

A couple of months ago the phone rang, and Tom said, "I'd like you to read my play."

I said that I didn't want to read it because I wanted to see it first. Your mother and I had already booked tickets to London, and we went to an early preview of *Leopoldstadt.*

He said, "I'd like you to know that I thought of you when I wrote this play."

I should have asked him, "Can I have that in writing, please?"

Well, to be peripherally involved somehow in a great playwright's effort is an honor. I think *Leopoldstadt* is a master work. It is a compelling play and also the idea that Stoppard has acknowledged, at age eighty-one, that he's a Jew is an extraordinary revelation.

He told me his childhood story a while ago. His mother, brother and father, who was a doctor, left Czechoslovakia to escape the Nazis. His family was Jewish but secular, and they escaped to Singapore. When they got to Singapore, they had to leave again because the Japanese were coming—this is World War II. The mother and the two boys went to India and the father would join them later. They never heard from the father again.

Five or six years go by, and the mother remarries Major Stoppard of the British Army. In effect he's kind of a bigot about everything that isn't British. They go back to England after the war, and Stoppard grows up as an Englishman. There was no mention of anything Jewish or of any extended family. Evidently, at some point he went back to the Czech Republic and discovered that one of his mother's sisters is still alive. She survived the camps and has children, and Tom learned that he has cousins, and also that his grandparents were orthodox Jews, and they were all killed in Auschwitz. I don't know the details of it, but over the years he does this research. Out of this comes *Leopoldstadt* and it's remarkable. *Leopoldstadt* is a ghetto in Vienna, and the play is a chronicle of that ghetto and a sort of fictional documentary of his family.

When playwrights get to be eighty, they are mostly forgotten, but he's written one of his great plays. The last twenty minutes of this play are as good and revealing as ever. Since I know the playwright and the personal trip he has made, I was overwhelmed. What he says in the play is stunning and intelligent and he says it in theatrical terms. He's a genius.

So for me, for posterity, it justifies in many respects what I did in my life. I'm not the writer, I'm not the director, or the actor or the dancer. I sit on the periphery, on the sidelines, and if you can affect anything meaningfully as a producer then you feel you are a participant. It justifies your life. To be a participant with arguably the best playwright in the English language is...

The most important thing is when Tom said, "I'd like you to read my play."

That was worth all the Tony Awards. It's only between you and me and your mother and my children that we know that. You don't take an ad out and say, "Look who I am!" [Speaking to me] You know, it's as if I gave Jerome Robbins a few steps. Ya know, "Jerry! Do this. I don't like the plié in that moment."

So if you add up my relationship with Neil Simon and my relationship with Tom Stoppard, it's okay. It's satisfactory. The acknowledgement that you participated. You read books now, "He was a friend of Beethoven!" Well, I am friends with Tom Stoppard, Athol Fugard, and Neil Simon, and I had some input. It was good. It's not a substitute for creativity, but for me it is fulfilling, and it's the best I got.

ACKNOWLEDGEMENTS

Thank you, Dad, for sharing your stories with me.
A big thanks to my editors, Michael Denneny and Kelly Davis. Thank you for understanding the significance of this piece and for honoring my father's voice. Your experience and professionalism brought my memoir to a whole new level.
To my cover artist, Caitlin B. Alexander, thank you for your artistry and for capturing a beautiful moment with my father on my book cover!
And lastly, thank you to both my parents, Manny and Lani, and my husband, Simon, for your constant love and support and for reading every word that I write.

ABOUT THE AUTHOR

Jessica Azenberg was born and raised in New York City. After graduating with a B.F.A. in Dance from The Boston Conservatory, Jessica performed as a dancer in many musicals across the country. She has also been teaching dance in New York City for the past eleven years. She now lives in Riverdale, New York, with her husband, Simon, and two adorable cats, Scout and Thomas. Jessica loves to spend her time writing the day away or reading a delectable murder mystery.

Made in United States
North Haven, CT
28 September 2022

24665416R00082